It's Not about the Fish
A Memoir

Bryan McMurry

ISBN Number: 978-0-9826120-0-2

Cover Design By: IntroBang! Inc.

Book Design By: Lisa Corcoran

Author Photograph: John Engstrom

Publisher: MC Squared

January 2010 Print On Demand By:
Lightning Source, INC., U.S.
246 Heil Quaker Blvd.
La Vergne, TN 37086 USA

HEALING WATERS
FLY FISHING

A portion of the profits from the sale of this book goes to supporting Project Healing Waters Fly Fishing's vision and noble mission of serving disabled active military service personnel and veterans.

Project Healing Waters Fly Fishing, Inc.^{SM} is dedicated to the physical and emotional rehabilitation of disabled active military service personnel and veterans through fly fishing and fly tying education and outings. Initiated and conducted by members of the Federation of Fly Fishers and Trout Unlimited, Project Healing Waters Fly Fishing, Inc. ^{SM} serves military personnel who have been wounded, injured, or disabled to aid their physical and emotional recovery by introducing or rebuilding the skills of fly fishing and fly tying and by using and enjoying these skills on fishing outings and as lifelong recreation.

Project Healing Waters Fly Fishing, Inc.^{SM} strives to effectively serve the deserving past and present members of our armed forces who have made great sacrifices in the service of our Nation. The project operates nationwide, offering its services and programs to active military personnel and veterans in Department of Defense and Department of Veterans Affair's hospitals throughout the country.

The project's program provides basic fly fishing, fly casting, fly tying and rod building classes and clinics for wounded and injured personnel ranging from beginners to those with prior fly fishing and tying experience who are adapting their skills to their new abilities. All activities and services are provided to the participants at no cost. Fly fishing and tying equipment and materials are provided to the participants, including equipment that accommodates their special needs.

Come help "serve those who have served" and be moved. To learn more about Project Healing Waters Fly Fishing, Inc.^{SM} go to **www. projecthealingwaters.org.**

Acknowledgements

Saying that fly-fishing saved my life is as much an overstatement as saying it changed my life is an understatement. The fact that you are holding this book is a testament to that change. Becoming an author wasn't even a blip on my radar screen until fly-fishing became a part of my life. Little did I know that what began on a quaint Montana creek, would launch me on a journey leading to life's single truth and the secret to all happiness.

My friend, Lex Gamblin, to whom I am forever indebted, and you will read about, gave me a gift that provided a new perspective to a life that began on a hardscrabble ranch too small to survive.

My wife, Roberta, knew the secret all along; she just assumed I did too, so her helping me in that regard was unconscious, but no less significant. She however has been my inspiration for twenty three years. Her unquestionable love, enormous capacity for understanding, unyielding support and constant encouragement are life's foundation. Fortunately, these same traits are enjoyed by our two daughters, Megan and Erin. They're constant reminders of the spirit of youth and have brought a joy to my life comparable to no other.

Too numerous to mention, many people have offered encouragement, advice, and valuable critique, and contributed to my spiritual evolution. Some of them you will read about in the pages to follow, but the most important one is absent, my editor, Carol Thoma, who works with A-1 Editing Services, LLC. She is absent only in name, but I assure you, she is there. Like finding a diamond in the desert—Carol lives in Arizona—I was surprised by her talent and passion for editing. She transformed incoherent thought, nonsensical babbling, dreadful spelling, and horrific grammar into a finished and entertaining manuscript worthy of publishing. Her insights and female perspective were invaluable and I cannot thank her enough.

I especially thank Bob Knutson and Debbie Strane, owners of Introbang, a creative marketing services company, for creating the cover design for this book. And finally my deepest thanks to Jim and Sondra Whitt of Purpose Unlimited for helping me begin living a more purpose driven life.

As for the rest of you that have contributed to my life in some form or fashion, you know who you are. Thank you.

Caveat homo unius libri

Our mistresses are many, and they live in the streams that hold trout. They are the nymphs who feed the trout with their namesakes because they know that mortal men, fly fishermen in pursuit of the trout, will come and feed their spirit, making them whole.

Prologue

I couldn't see squat! The early morning sunlight reflecting off the water at a low angle, created a wicked glare. Despite my dark, polarized sunglasses, I could feel the cataracts forming. Fishing the middle of the river required staring directly into that sun; I needed a welding helmet.

Leafless alders choked the west bank. Their red branches hanging out over the water brushed against me as I waded upstream toward a cascading riffle. The wading was easy in the shallow water, but the small gravel was slippery, so I reached out and grabbed the alder branches to steady myself. The alder buds, swollen hard with soon-to-emerge spring leaves, felt like the tips of drumsticks.

As I looked upriver—north—the sun continued to pester me, knifing in on my right side behind the lens of my sunglasses. I adjusted my cap, cocking it exaggeratedly low on the right side of my head to shade my eyes from the direct sunlight. The reflection from the water's surface was still a bitch, but by squinting, I could see into the water about forty feet ahead of me.

The water was clear, but lightly tannin stained from draining the muskeg country—land covered with peat-like plant matter—of the upper reaches. The shallow water where I waded resembled weak iced tea; the deeper water, considerably darker, was reminiscent of a stoutly brewed Earl Gray.

Upstream, about thirty feet out from the alders, the water looked lighter, evidence of a shallow-water shelf. The darker band of water between the shelf and the alders was a trough or small channel likely to hold fish, around which I could formulate a plan.

Half the fun of fly-fishing is strategizing to determine the best tactics to fish a particular piece of water. The planning creates anticipation, adding to the excitement.

From the shelf, the sun at my back, I thought it would be easy to spot the long, straight silhouette of a steelhead against the backdrop of small, round, light brown stones on the river bottom. *Shallow wading, the sun to my advantage, nothing to obstruct the backcast,* I thought. *This is a no brainer.*

I figured that fishing the channel up to the steeper, cascading riffle would take an hour or so. By then the sun would be high enough that I could face east, with minimum eye damage, and fish the main body of the river, working my way back downstream. *Good plan,* I concluded.

As I waded across the knee-deep tail end of the trough and up onto the shelf, the splashy sounds from the cascading riffle upstream grew louder. I straightened my cap, and, wading slowly upstream in nearly knee-deep water, stared intently into the bronze-colored channel. The bright morning sun, which felt warm on my back, threw my shadow nearly to the trough and illuminated the rocky bottom. *If I can't see a fish in there, I might as well go home,* I thought.

I eased upstream, stopping every three or four steps to peruse the four-foot-deep trough and the shallower water near the bank. Since the trough darkened as it deepened, I took my time, not wanting to miss any fish that might be lying on the bottom.

As I looked upstream to get a feel for how much farther the trough extended, something near the alders caught my eye. At first, the dark shadow, about seventy-five feet upstream, looked like a submerged alder branch undulating in the water. *That's probably not a fish,* I thought. Yet I found myself cautiously wading upstream, my eyes fixated on the dark, linear form.

Is that a branch? I thought. *Could it be a fish? No.*

Forgetting about the channel, I stopped, leaned forward slightly, and squinted to bring the dark, shadowy form into focus. Suddenly, my body tightened! *Holy smokes, that's a fish!* Not six feet out from the alders, at the upstream edge of the trough, in two and a half feet of water, was the biggest steelhead I'd ever seen. Suddenly paralyzed, my gut hollow, I fixated on the shadowy outline. *Is this a dream?* I closed my eyes, shook my head, and looked again. *Still there!*

Wading turned to stalking. I no longer noticed the water pressing against my shins. Like a cat hunting a field mouse, I kept my eyes on the long dark shadow, fearing that looking away would somehow cause it to disappear. I slipped into questioning mode. *Why is a huge fish alone in shallow water?* If it was a female—and I was sure it was—she could be building a redd (a nest to lay eggs in), but she wasn't turning on her side, beating the river bottom with her tail to furrow the gravel. She was upright, lazily waving her tail to maintain her position.

Slowly and deliberately I moved, as quietly as the flowing water allowed, and the hunt continued. *Is she waiting for a big buck to show up to complete the mating ritual?* I doubted it because during the spawning season, the bucks stay very close to the hens. In fact, a number of suitors usually beleaguer the female until the alpha male takes his rightful place. I stopped, leaned forward, staring fixedly. If a male was there, I couldn't see him. *Damn, she's big!*

Still fifty feet downstream from her, I began moving again, very slowly. Big fish in shallow water are very spooky, and it wouldn't take much to send this fish rocketing to deeper water. Doubts crept into my mind as I stalked closer. *There's no way this fish is going to stay there,* I thought. And, yet, she *was* still there, less than fifty feet away, and with every step, closer still.

Doubts are often rationalizations from a fear of failure, inherently negative, like the fear of rejection that keeps middle school boys from asking a pretty girl to dance with them, leaving the poor girl to stand around all night. My daddy always told me, "Son, if you want a cookie, ask for a cookie!" Consequently, I danced with all the girls—and I was about to ask this big hen to two-step.

Now only thirty feet downstream from the fish, I realized that she was well over thirty inches. She was deep sided and from this angle looked like a three-foot-long, two-by-ten-inch plank in the water. *She's at least fifteen pounds,* I thought. My left hand—the one holding the rod—began to tremble. I took a deep breath, exhaled loudly, and tried to shake out the tension.

I removed my egg pattern fly from the hook keeper, let it drag in the water, and then pulled a few feet of floating fly line from the reel with one hand while I shook the slack out through the rod tip with the other. Hands shaking, I changed the fluorescent orange strike indicator to a small white one, placing it about three feet above the egg pattern fly. The white strike indicator would look more like a bubble floating on the surface, less likely than the fluorescent orange one to spook an already wary fish—in theory. Holding the leader in my right hand and examining my strike indicator and hook setup, I took another deep breath and exhaled slowly.

I had rigged up with the typical cordlike floating fly line, my preferred method for steelheading. Some tight line anglers who used the more conventional monofilament line often refer to my method as "throwing the rope." Growing up on a ranch and having dragged countless calves to the branding fire, I viewed that rope analogy with a degree of reverence. *What better way for a cowboy to catch things than with a rope?* I remember thinking.

I stood at about a forty-five degree angle twenty feet downstream from her, which made the distance to her just over twenty-eight feet. To land the fly and indicator fifteen feet upstream from her would require about a forty-foot cast; the Pythagorean Theorem ($A^2 + B^2 = C^2$) applied to fly-fishing. Who says trigonometry was a waste of time?

I could see her clearly now. In the stained water, her bright silver side shone gold. The short snout and small mouth told me that it was indeed a hen—a monster hen! I had dreamed about this very moment. Light-headed, visibly shaking, my stomach knotted, I had to force deep breaths.

My position was perfect—low profile and low angle relative to the fish, the sun behind me and off my right shoulder. She had no idea I was there. Pointing the rod downstream and still looking at the fish, I slowly pulled line from the reel, letting the tow from the flowing water pull it through the rod tip. I shot a quick look downstream; about fifty feet of bright yellow fly line was floating straight below me. I bowed and rolled my shoulders to loosen up one last time. I was ready!

I looked back at the fish, took in a long, deep breath, and lifted my rod, which flexed from the pull of the water on the line as it lifted off the surface below me. I could no longer hear the splashy riffle upstream, and my periphery blurred; I could see only a ten-foot circle around the fish. The muscles in my right arm tightened. Just about to snap the rod forward, a voice in my head stopped me. *You've only been fly-fishing for six years. What right do you have to cast to a magnificent fish like this?*

A fair question, I suppose, but to answer it, I'll need to start at the beginning.

Chapter 1

Rock Creek

I've been fascinated by fly-fishing since my father showed me his old South Bend bamboo rod and the Martin automatic reel when I was 12. He'd carried that rod and reel when he was a young man running a pack string (five mules packed with gear) out of the Mineral King pack station into the wilderness areas of Sequoia and Kings Canyon National Parks during the early 1940s.

He often told me stories about "packing" people from all walks of life into the "high country," as he called it, to enjoy the wilderness and pursue the geographically specific, and consequently rare, golden trout. In 1947, when the golden trout became the state fish of California, those two parks were the only places on earth where it was known to exist.

Found at high elevations, golden trout are native to a small section of the Kern Plateau in the southern Sierra Nevada but, through introduction, the species now thrives in other high-mountain streams in the western United States. Dad told me he had caught them as high as ten thousand feet above sea level. Like many taxonomists, Dad considered the golden trout a specific species, *Oncorhynchus aguabonita*. However, over the years biologists changed the Linnaean classification of the golden trout to a subspecies of the rainbow trout, *Oncorhynchus mykiss aguabonita*.

While my father and I gathered cattle in the high country of the Cascade Range in Northern California, he often told me stories about fishing the Sierra high country. Crossing a creek or riding up on a lake would bring the memories flooding back to him.

One of his favorite stories was of three fly-fishing nuns who hired my dad to pack them into Kings Canyon. Dad said he knew he was in for a good trip when he began packing supplies into the panniers—bags or boxes that hang on either side of the packsaddle— and there were six bottles of whiskey for a five-day trip. "Just a little snake bite medicine," one nun told him with a sly wink.

The first night in camp the nuns broke out the whiskey and were "hootin' and hollerin'" well past midnight according to dad. My dad was a hell of a storyteller, but he said he was no match for those nuns. He woke up the next morning in his bedroll, not remembering how he got there. The nuns were drinking coffee and frying bacon as if it were just another day at the basilica. He said they caught a lot of fish and it was the most fun he had ever had on a pack trip.

Growing up in Siskiyou County, one of three California counties that border Oregon, I should have had many fly-fishing opportunities, too, but my father was too busy trying to scratch out a living on a small ranch to teach me the sport when I was young. Later, after I entered high school, I developed other interests and social ties, and my quest for independence strained our relationship.

My dad often challenged what he viewed as my pointless activities and questionable associations. When I challenged him to recollect the impulsiveness of his own youth, he often succumbed to selective amnesia, dismissing his youthful escapades as a passing phase. "Things were different back then," he proclaimed. Although he couldn't convince me to share his view, he obviously saw my actions as stumbling around, lost in the fog of youth. In vain, he tried to convince me that the pothole-littered path I was traveling led nowhere. That didn't help.

Like that of most teenagers, my frontal cortex, the part of the brain responsible for planning and reasoning, wasn't fully developed. Poor judgment and operating without a plan were as much a part of normal adolescent behavior in the early 1970s as they are today. Kids are still the same. At the time, we didn't realize the cause of this behavior. My father just referred to my lack of planning and questionable judgment as being hail damaged.

While my dad had already negotiated the path around the potholes of adolescence, he didn't intend to relive them vicariously. Those experiences he had lived through had made him the man he was, and I think, deep down, he knew that it was time to let me find my own path to becoming a man. Eventually, you need to grow up on your own.

This approach worked equally well with daughters. My wife, Roberta (Bert), and I raised two daughters with unconditional love and a great deal of good fortune. We let them make their own choices—within reason, of course. I told them simply, "Your choices can result in situations that your daddy can't get you out of, no matter how badly I might want to." A sobering thought, I hoped, and little against which to rebel. Apparently, assigning the responsibility of their actions to them worked.

As a kid, I spent springtime working calves on our ranch and the neighboring ranches and repairing fences in the high country where we pastured the cows and their calves during the summer months. In late spring, on horseback, we'd drive cows and calves up the mountain to turn them out onto their summer range. During the summer, we baled hay and harvested grain, prepared 4-H steer and hog projects for the county fair, and enjoyed an occasional rodeo.

In fall, when my brother, sister, and I were back in school, my dad, my brother, and I spent the weekends gathering cattle off the summer range, cutting our winter firewood, butchering a fat calf and a few hogs, and, occasionally, deer hunting. If we were lucky, we might find time to chase a salmon or a steelhead when the fish returned to the river to spawn, but I never did it with a fly rod. Mostly, we fished by bouncing roe (cured salmon eggs tied in cheesecloth sacks) along the bottom of the Klamath River between the dam at Iron Gate Reservoir and the Klamathon Bridge.

Wintertime meant feeding cows the hay we'd spent all summer baling, as well as working on equipment and calving heifers. On the weekends we would head to the Klamath River to fish for winter steelhead. Soon, it was spring, and the entire process began again.

We didn't make much money, but it was a great way to grow up. As kids, we didn't care if we had a pot to piss in or a window to throw it out of; we grew up happy and thankful for what we had. My sister and brother-in-law decided to raise their family on a ranch in Siskiyou County, but a twist of fate —the cattle market crash in 1973—left little hope of owning a ranch and sent me in another direction.

With no money and little prospects, I joined the Army to take advantage of the benefits offered through the GI Bill. Ultimately, those benefits afforded me the chance to attend college, eventually earning graduate degrees in animal science from Texas A&M. In 1992 I joined the animal nutrition division at Cargill, Inc. and in 1999 became the beef brand manager.

Managing Cargill's beef nutrition products, programs, and services meant traveling into cattle country, which, coincidentally, is often fly-fishing country as well. On one of those trips, I found myself standing on the edge of Rock Creek, holding a fiberglass fly rod and my daddy's old Martin reel.

A tributary that joins the Yellowstone River near Laurel, Montana, Rock Creek originates in the Absaroka-Beartooth Wilderness Area in the Gallatin National Forest. After flowing through rugged, steep timber country for eighteen miles, the stream flattens out as it leaves Red Lodge, a quaint little town halfway between Billings and the northeast entrance to Yellowstone National Park.

About a mile after turning west and running under Highway 212, the creek flows along the west side of a pastured valley dotted with ranch houses. For a five-mile stretch, Rock Creek hugs a low, steep, rocky rim that, over time, has supplied the creek with large rocks that create great holding water for trout. Not far from Boyd, Montana, the stream meanders back into the middle of the valley where it remains until it merges with the Yellowstone River.

One sunny morning in July 2000, I drove through Boyd to meet my friend, and now long-time fishing partner, Lex Gamblin, who was about to take on the role of fly-fishing guide and give me my first official fly-fishing lesson. Lex owned a house near Rock Creek, about a mile and a half from Boyd.

Some years earlier, I had bought the fiberglass rod thinking that someday I would learn to fly-fish. That day had finally come. The rod wasn't a particularly good one, but it was substantially better than my casting ability.

Earlier, before we walked down the quarter-mile of gravel road from his house to the creek, Lex gave me a lesson on the lawn in his front yard. He told me that casting with a fly rod was nothing like using other types of rods. Because the weight is in the line, fly casting requires a different casting stroke than spin casting where the weight is on the end of the leader. Technique and timing, not strength and power, control the line and create line speed, translating into casting distance and accuracy.

We arrived at the creek a little before noon. Fully outfitted in a new pair of waders and a vest from which dangled all the necessary tools of the fly-fishing trade, I was ready to catch my first trout on a fly rod.

I flailed around at the edge of Rock Creek for several minutes, whipping the line back and forth. About the time I'd get twenty feet or so of line out, the line would collapse and become draped around my shoulders with the hook stuck in my shirt. At first, I expected Lex to walk back to the house, shaking his head in obvious wonder. Instead, he was having a good laugh at my expense. Finally, after a particularly pitiful attempt at casting ended with the fly line hanging on my left ear, I looked over at Lex, who was bent over with his hands on his knees, laughing.

"A hell of a coach you are," I hollered. "Throw me a frickin' bone here!"

"Okay," he said. "Now that I've had my laugh for the day, let's get serious. You're making the classic mistake, allowing your wrist to break like you're casting a spinning rod and not hesitating enough on the backcast to allow the rod to load properly." Loading the rod, he explained, means getting the rod to flex under the weight of the line as the line extends behind you on the backcast.

After a few minutes of demonstration, he made casting look easier than it really was and me look like a bumbling idiot. In the process of "teaching" me, he caught a nice rainbow in the twelve-inch range. Adding insult to injury, he asked me to net the fish for him and then handed me back the rod.

"See, it's easy," he snickered.

Sorry bastard.

"If it wasn't for the fact that you have teeth in your mouth, you'd be the perfect horse's ass," was the best retort I could muster. At least, I knew how to remove a hook from a fish. I released the silvery rainbow, which shot back into the clear depths of the creek.

After fifteen minutes or so, I could get the line out about twenty-five feet. Granted, it usually wasn't where I wanted it and almost never where Lex wanted it, but it was at least getting out. Lex suggested I practice there while he went downstream to look for some fish.

About fifteen minutes later, Lex came walking back upstream. "How ya doin'?" he asked as he walked by me.

"I think I'm starting to get the hang of it," I replied.

Lex walked about twenty feet upstream from me. He stepped up on a large rock half buried in the fist-sized gravel about fifteen feet from the edge of the creek and began looking at the water. "There's a fish right there; see him?" he said, pointing. "Just cast to the middle of the creek about where that little willow branch is hanging over."

I floundered around, stepped on the slack part of the line that was lying at my feet, and then got my line hung up in the brush behind me. I looked up and saw Lex standing with his hands on his hips, looking utterly disgusted.

"Are you done screwing around now?" he quipped.

"No," I said. "You don't look aggravated enough."

"I may be closer than you think," he replied.

Finally, I got everything untangled and took a position where my backcast would travel straight downstream to stay out of the streamside foliage. Earlier, Lex had recommended a Prince Nymph and a tan Gold-Ribbed Hare's Ear—flies that resemble insects in the nymph stage fished below the surface of the water—placed about eighteen inches apart and supervised me as I tied them on. Then he had me place a round, fluorescent strike indicator—a small float that helps you detect when a fish has taken your fly—about six feet up the leader from the bottom fly. Surprisingly, the entire rig was still intact after all the trouble I'd been having.

I managed to get close to where Lex wanted me to cast but left too much slack on the water. As I was trying to gather up the slack in my line, Lex said, "Lift your rod."

"What?" I asked.

"A trout took one of your nymphs," he said.

"Oh, bullshit!" I exclaimed.

"You didn't see him flash?"

"I was too busy trying to gather slack."

"Okay, let's try this again, only this time I want you to hold your backcast after you stop to the count of one thousand one and then drive it forward with your arm, not your wrist. Abruptly stop your forward motion when the rod is at about a forty-five degree angle in front of you. The instant you stop the forward motion, allow the line in your left hand to slide through as your line, leader, and flies begin to straighten out in front of you. Then point the rod tip at the spot on the water where you want the flies to land. When the indicator hits the water, hook the line in your left hand to the trigger finger on your right hand. Then, begin pulling the line through your trigger finger with your left hand to take up the slack in the line floating on the water."

The next cast felt a little awkward because I was trying to remember everything, but the indicator actually landed near where I wanted it. I had just started stripping line when Lex hollered, "There he is! Lift your rod!"

By the time I had lifted the rod, the fish was gone.

"Didn't you see that rainbow come up?" he asked.

"No."

"Did you see the silver flash as he turned away?"

"No."

"Are those eyes in your head or just two sheep turds in a pan of buttermilk? When was the last time you had your eyes checked?"

"I can see your dough ass!"

"Well, you didn't buy that fishing license to catch me."

"Keep in mind that the season is always open on fat-ass Irishmen, and it's catch-as-catch-can!"

"Let me see those sunglasses," Lex said, jumping off the rock and walking over to me.

I was wearing a pair of Ray-Ban Aviators that I'd had for years. Their UV protection was as good as any, but they were designed for flying, not fishing.

"Are these glasses polarized?" Lex asked as I handed them to him.

"I don't think so," I replied.

Lex took one look through them and said, "Well, you may have a good excuse for not seeing the fish, but it doesn't excuse you from being asleep at the switch. When I say 'lift your rod,' I don't mean when you get around to it. I mean now!" He handed the sunglasses back to me. "This time, keep your eye on the strike indicator. If it stops, hesitates, moves sideways, or does anything unusual, just lift the rod. There's a good chance that a fish is on the other end."

I nodded but said nothing as Lex climbed back up on his pedestal. "There are more fish further up the run, so step up about ten feet," Lex said, folding his arms like Yul Brynner in *The King and I*.

"Now cast into the middle of the run, get the slack out, and watch the indicator," he ordered. "Et cetera, et cetera, et cetera," he added in his best Yul Brynner accent.

I still had to think too much about casting technique. I could tell that Lex was growing impatient, but he clearly enjoyed watching me fumble around and having a good laugh at my expense. I knew he wouldn't pass up an opportunity to get more good stories that he could, and all too often would, copiously embellish with only the sliver of an audience.

I let go another cast into the middle of the choppy run and began to strip in line as the indicator drifted back toward me.

"Strip faster," Lex suggested.

I had started to follow orders when Lex shouted, "Lift your rod!" just as the indicator went completely under water.

I couldn't believe it and thought I was hung up on the bottom. I lifted the rod tip and felt something shaking on the other end, so I pulled a little harder. The line came shooting back toward me, most of it falling limp over me. "I felt the fish pull back!" I shouted.

"No shit?" Lex asked.

"No shit!" I exclaimed, "I felt him—"

"I'll be damned!" Lex interrupted, laughing, "The idea is to get the fish to pull back for a little while longer."

As I cautiously lifted the line from around me, being careful not to get a hook stuck in my shirt, he chuckled, "Just how long did you think that fish would keep that indicator under the surface before he figured out something was wrong and spit your bug out? Maybe if he pulls your rod tip under the water, you'll get it?"

"Just how well do you suppose your underwear will fit with this fly rod sticking out of your ass?" I asked.

Lex laughed hard and bent over. That got me to laughing, too.

"Damn," he howled, taking off his glasses to wipe his eyes. "My stomach hurts!" Standing up straight, he huffed, "All this instruction is making me thirsty. I need a beer." I was still trying to unhook one of the nymphs from my fishing vest.

Lex reached into his shirt pocket, and pulled out a can of Skoal. "Damn it, man!" he said, giving the can a couple of raps into his left palm. "Would you hurry up and catch a damn fish so we can go back to the house and get some lunch and a cold beer?" He took a dip of tobacco and returned the can to his pocket. "Let me know when you're ready to quit screwing around."

Walking crouched and watching the water, Lex eased into a new position, upstream from the big rock.

"Putting the sneak on them?" I asked.

"These fish don't know my whereabouts," he explained, looking back with a twinkle in his eye. "Step up a bit and cast as far up as you can."

"You're the epitome of stealth," I replied as I stepped up another three to four steps, cast as far as I could, and began stripping.

"Now, as the indicator approaches, slowly raise your rod to lift the line off the water. Then, as the indicator passes you and continues downstream, slowly lower your rod tip and place the line back on the water. That increases the length of your drift."

"Hey, that's pretty cool," I said as the strike indicator drifted by.

"When the line tightens at the end of the drift, keep your rod tip pointed at the indicator and let the line tighten in the current and your bugs swing up from the bottom naturally," Lex continued. "It will look like a bug coming up to hatch, and a fish will sometimes whack it hard. Fish know that they have to strike quickly to capture emerging bugs and will often hook themselves before you even lift the rod. And as slow as you are, you'll need all the help you can get."

After a few more drifts, it was getting a little easier to execute the cast and subsequently manage the drift.

"Okay, step up another four or five steps," Lex said. "Now be ready. There are fish at the head of the run." He pointed to a spot where large rocks narrowed the stream flow, an ideal holding spot for trout.

The pause on the backcast seemed long and exaggerated, but, for the first time, I actually felt the pull of the line as the rod loaded behind me. I shot my arm forward, and the line in front of me seemed to hang suspended in the air above the run. The bugs landed first, closely followed by the indicator, and then the fly line settled on the surface in a nearly straight line.

"Not bad! There may be hope for you yet!" shouted Lex as I hooked the line in my trigger finger and began stripping.

I locked onto that indicator like a cat ready to pounce. Time slowed to a crawl. Then it happened. The indicator hesitated subtly in the current. Unconsciously, my right hand shot up, even before Lex said, "There he is, son! You got him!"

The trout pulled hard, shook repeatedly, and then jumped about two feet out of the water several times. I was afraid he would get off.

"Get him on the reel," Lex shouted. The lever was right under my pinky finger and, when I applied just a bit of pressure, all the slack zipped back onto the reel. The fish settled into the run.

"Keep a little pressure on him," Lex said, walking toward me to grab the net clipped to a ring just under the collar on the back of my fly vest.

The fish fought for another minute or two and then rolled onto the water's surface in front of me as Lex netted him. He reached out to shake my hand and said, "Congratulations! Your first Montana trout on a fly rod."

"Thanks," I replied. "That was pretty cool."

After Lex took a picture of me with my shiny, silver, thirteen-inch trophy, I released it back into Rock Creek and it shot off into the clear, cool depths. I rinsed my hands in the creek, stood up, and pressed the lever that reels in the line, which zipped back onto the reel, and then hooked the bottom fly in the hook keeper above the rod handle.

"Let's get a bite to eat," said Lex.

I started to say, "Hey, I really appreciate—"

"I'm thirsty," Lex interrupted. "Can we get that beer now?"

"I'm trying to tell you—"

"I'm hungry and thirsty!" he said as he turned to head for the house. "That comedy routine you put on beside the creek dehydrated me."

"Instructing dehydrates you?" I asked.

"No, laughing at your pathetic ass dehydrates me," he said over his shoulder. "I'm hungry because it took you half a damn day to catch your first fish on a fly rod."

"If you were worth a shit as a guide, it wouldn't have taken so long," I said, hurrying to catch up.

"Worth a shit as a guide?" he shot back. "Guiding you is like guiding Barney Fife. One-bullet Barney. It's a good thing that was a fly rod in your hand and not a pistol; you might have shot yourself in the foot."

"You puss-gutted son of a bitch, guiding is more than standing on a rock barking orders and giving people shit."

"Quit yakkin' and come on. I need a beer! Hell, after putting up with you all day, I may have to break out the scotch."

As I trotted up beside Lex, I stuck out my hand. "Thanks," I said. "This meant a lot to me."

"Any time, buddy," Lex replied as he shook my hand. "Now it's official," he proclaimed loudly. "Women love him—fish fear him!"

My transition from incompetence to competence had begun. All I needed now was experience, like the fly-fishing experiences my father had shared with me as we rode the range.

Chapter 2

Competence

Even though it didn't seem that cold outside, steam was slowly rising from the little holes in the lids of the two extra large coffees I was carrying as I walked to the fueling island of the local convenience store. Economists may categorize coffee as nonessential, more of a luxury than a necessity, but try explaining that to most fishermen during the early morning hours of a fishing trip.

Many fly fishers I know would point out that without coffee early in the morning, there would be no fishing. On the rare occasion that economic theory enters your mind at dawn, that first euphoric sip scatters those errant thoughts like spooked trout in a clear, shallow stream. *No doubt about it,* I thought. *Coffee is one of the necessities of life.*

Reasonably priced coffee at convenience stores is an effective tactic to get consumers into the store. However, the many other nonessential items, conveniently placed where we must walk right past them on the way to the coffee, are high profit margin goods often purchased on impulse. The convenience of satisfying our impulses and our willingness to buy things that we probably don't need, constitutes the Stop-N-Rob business model. Purchasing these impulse items is not rational, but nobody's holding a gun to our heads.

The reality, according to behavioral economists, is that people don't act rationally; instead, we tend to focus on the present and discount the future. The pleasure of doing something now out-weighs the pleasure of delayed gratification. Conversely, we pro-crastinate because we think that the pain of doing something we don't like is greater today than it will be in the future, which we perceive, paradoxically, as both less pleasurable and less painful than the present. Convenience store merchandising counts on our choosing to enjoy a doughnut today and ignoring the nutritional consequences that won't show up until later.

Approaching the pickup with these thoughts in mind, I sipped my coffee through the little hole in the spill-proof lid. "Shit, that's hot!" I said to myself as I squinted, pulled up my head, and tweaked it to one side all in one motion.

"Watch out! That coffee is hot!" Lex said, looking up from washing the windshield and laughing.

"Figured that out on my own," I replied. As the handle on the fuel nozzle tripped and shut off with a loud click, I added, "Want me to drive?"

"Sure." He hung up the nozzle, pulled off the receipt, and we traded seats.

The first rays of direct sunlight had yet to break over the Conti-nental Divide and hit the town of Last Chance, Idaho, as we pulled onto Highway 20, heading north.

Last Chance is on the Henry's Fork of the Snake River. We had fished the upper Henry's Fork, floating in our pontoon boats, from Island Park to Last Chance the day before with little success. About halfway through the canyon of the upper stretch, a thunder-storm had blown in, forcing us to take refuge on shore for a good thirty minutes while the cumulonimbus clouds performed one of nature's spectacular light-and-sound shows. Although the odds of lightning striking you are remote—one in about 576,000 strikes,

according to Wikipedia—its 50,000 degree Fahrenheit temperatures and 300 million volts of electricity can ruin a fishing trip in
literally an instant. We lost two cows to a single lightning strike on
the ranch one summer. We found the cows dead within ten feet of
one another, grass still hanging out of their mouths.

Although the lightning had subsided, it was still raining hard
when we launched the boats to continue downstream. We rowed
hard downstream the rest of the way while the rain splattered on the
river like a cow peeing on a flat rock. The rain stopped as abruptly
as it had begun about a quarter mile from the "takeout"— the term
for a boat launch at the end of a drift—near town. Despite being
rained out and fishless, we were by no means broken men. The
restaurant in town had cold beer.

Remembering that experience as I sipped my coffee and looked
out the windshield at the sky, I hoped that this day's fishing would
be better. Sunlight struggled to appear through the thick fir forest that lined the highway. Lex's coffee had remained in the cup
holder since we first pulled onto the highway and he looked as
though he was settling into the passenger seat for a little nap. He
hadn't said a word for a couple of miles, and when he reclined the
seat, I knew it was over.

Our destination was Yellowstone Park, where we intended to
see what angling opportunities might present themselves on the
upper Yellowstone River. Although the tourists hit many of the
park's waters hard, most don't get far from the parking areas, so if
you're willing to hike a bit, you can find relatively secluded water
that has somewhat less educated fish.

It's very challenging to find a big trout in Yellowstone Park
that doesn't have a PhD in counter tactical fly-fishing. Big trout are
old trout, and—unlike some people I've encountered—they don't
get to be old being fools.

These big, savvy trout, which have seen every imaginable bug imitation thrown at them under a variety of conditions, will often reject even perfectly drifted flies. Remember, this is Yellowstone, the most upscale environment for a fish. These older and wiser fish, like folks with a house in the Hamptons, rarely stoop to haphazard dining. They can be downright snobbish, turning a blind eye to even the most delicate presentation of what most fish would consider an entomological hors d'oeuvre. You need a high level of fly-fishing competence or a good deal of luck to "hang a pig" (hook a big fish) on the upper Yellowstone. In most cases, you'll need both.

The tires hummed, creating an eerie rhythm as the three-quarter-ton Chevy pickup rolled through the morning mist. I set the cruise control and settled in for the drive, sipping the hot coffee carefully. Shooting a glance at Lex, who was lightly snoring, I remembered Rock Creek, two years earlier.

Since then, I had read and studied both the art and science of fly-fishing and applied the principles on the spring creeks in Wisconsin and Southeastern Minnesota. I felt a certain serene satisfaction as my abilities improved and my knowledge of fly-fishing's intricacies increased. I had fished the lower Yellowstone, Gallatin, and Madison Rivers several times, so I was beginning to build a repertoire of experiences.

Even though I had certainly achieved a higher level of competence since that day on Rock Creek, Lex was concerned that I might be falling prey to the believing-your-own-bullshit syndrome, which we all tend to do from time to time. I still had, and always will have, a lot to learn, which Lex was eager to point out.

"You're so green that if you stumbled off into the woods, a moose might eat you," he would say.

Fly-fishing in and of itself has a way of humbling us, and if it fails in that regard, we have our fly-fishing friends to remind us, usually at the most inopportune times.

Recalling the challenges of that first casting lesson on Rock Creek, I realized that there was simply too much information to process at one time. In fly-fishing, like many other skills, repetition is the key to learning. Unfortunately, I seemed to need a great deal more repetition than most people.

At least, I was now more competent in basic casting technique. According to *The Empathic Communicator* by W. S. Howell, learning any skill or discipline requires a journey through four stages: unconscious incompetence, conscious incompetence, conscious competence, and unconscious competence.

Unconscious incompetence occurs when you don't comprehend or know how to do something and you're unaware of your shortcoming. More simply, you don't know what you don't know. You are, in fact, ignorant of your ignorance. Not knowing what you're missing is the essence of the cliché, "Ignorance is bliss."

With conscience incompetence, you know that you lack understanding or knowledge but you have not yet addressed the shortfall. Again, more simply stated, you know what you don't know. In other words, you're aware of your ignorance or inability, and you can do something about it if you're so inclined. With the bliss of ignorance gone, you may realize what you've missed. From there, you can either rationalize and move on with life or realize that the previous ignorance was not so blissful after all and choose to become competent.

Consciously competent people know how to do something with varying degrees of skill. However, exhibiting this knowledge or skill requires conscious effort or attention. You know what you know, but you still have to think about how to do it, which makes your execution conspicuously inconsistent. Not surprisingly, most injuries or accidents in physically demanding or high-risk activities occur at this stage of learning, which is why auto insurance rates are so high for inexperienced drivers under twenty-five.

Unconscious competence comes after much practice and repetition. Demonstrating a skill or discussing a subject knowledgeably becomes second nature, requiring little or no conscious concentration. Even though "you don't know what you know" sounds like an odd description of this stage and should not to be confused with forgetting what you know, it's essentially accurate. You have, in fact, learned and put actions into your subconscious the same way a typist types without thinking about the location of the keys. The letter A becomes the pressing of the left pinky finger on the middle row of keys, and the conscious mind doesn't think about what the finger is doing.

Scientists refer to the physiological changes resulting from learning a physical activity that requires specialized muscle movements as "muscle memory." Of course, muscles don't have memories per se, but repeated activity strengthens and conditions them. In effect, muscle memory results from training your muscles and your brain simultaneously. If repetition and practice strengthens the connections between the brain and muscles, then the old adage "practice makes perfect" makes perfect sense.

For most of us, the first experience with muscle memory (after learning to walk) is learning to ride a bike. Very few people "forget" how to ride a bike once they have learned simply because the actions required for riding a bike became a permanent subconscious memory. Your brain still knows how to ride a bike even if you can't remember the last time you rode one. If you decide to try it, don't worry! Your muscles will remind you how long it's been.

Fly-casting requires you to use muscles that you don't normally exercise extensively, so you have to condition them to perform the action effectively. Experienced fly fishers like my friend Lex make casting look effortless, but for beginners, that effort is self-evident.

When I was learning, my arm and shoulder tired quickly and could be shot by lunchtime—providing, of course, that I made it to lunchtime before becoming frustrated, throwing the rod on the ground, and stomping off in total disgust. I learned fairly quickly that it helps if you can laugh at yourself and, more important, if you can tolerate your friends' laughing with you.

By the time of our Yellowstone trip, I could cast without conscious effort. Casting required no more thinking than walking. After countless hours of practice and some guidance from Lex, I could, "Just do it."

My subconscious mind had taken over, and my conscious mind was free to take on another task or train of thought. This process is perfectly normal for humans and usually harmless—unless the physical activity is driving a pickup and your conscious mind is daydreaming about, say, fly-fishing, while your fishing partner sleeps in the passenger seat.

If you daydream while you're driving, your subconscious mind apparently takes over the driving as your conscious mind dreams away the miles. Unfortunately, focusing on your daydream instead of your driving can cause you to drift onto the shoulder of the road or across the centerline. Fortunately, your conscious mind usually realizes that you're driving in time to avoid a jaws-of-life extraction from a car now worth little more than a moderately priced wristwatch.

These days, most roads have washboard-like grooves cut into the shoulders and along the center line that create a whirring vibration when they're crossed, startling errant drivers out of their daydreams. Even though I know that these grooves avert accidents and save lives, running over them still pisses me off.

Oh, shit!" I gasped, slamming on the brakes as a big mule deer doe suddenly appeared in the road.

The strange, synthetic rubbing sound of anti-lock brakes engaging filled the cab. Lex lurched forward into the shoulder strap of his seat belt, snapped from his slumber into the reality of the moment.

"Damn it, man!" Lex shouted as he reached for the dashboard, which the shoulder belt kept him from hitting.

No sooner had the doe appeared than she was gone across the opposite lane and over the embankment. I glanced in the mirror—nothing—gradually guided the truck to the shoulder of the road, and stopped.

Breathing rapidly, we sat in silence for a few seconds, waiting for our hearts to quit racing and our stomachs to return to their normal location. I took a long, deliberate deep breath and exhaled.

"You all right?" I asked, still half out of breath.

"That bitch scared the shit out of me!" Lex said.

"You? I think I might need some toilet paper."

I took another deep breath and then exhaled as I surveyed my faculties. Except for my trembling, everything seemed normal. I was beginning to come down from the adrenalin-induced excitement.

"Good time to purge some coffee," Lex decided aloud as he opened the passenger-side door.

Suddenly, that same urge topped my priority list, too.

Standing on the side of the highway watering the roadside vegetation, I remembered seeing the sign to Henry's Lake at the junction of Highway 87 some four miles back but nothing since. Unconscious competence had nearly brought our fishing trip to a literal screeching halt. I made the mistake of sharing that information with Lex.

"If you can't pay attention any better than that, I think I'll drive," Lex said as he started back to the pickup.

"Shut up and toss me that roll of toilet paper you keep in there," I shot back.

"I've got a man down here!" Lex shouted as he tossed me the half-full roll. "Should I call 911?"

"If I'm not back in ten minutes, call for a medivac!" I called over my shoulder as I did the green-apple quick step into the trees. "I might need some air support."

Lex was sitting in the passenger seat drinking his coffee when I got back to the truck. "We're about ten miles from Yellowstone," said Lex, "let's go."

The ranger shack at the West Yellowstone entrance is just east of the Montana community of the same name. We stopped in town just long enough to purchase sandwiches for lunch on the river. I drove slowly away from the ranger shack, my left arm hanging out of the window, staring at my surroundings in complete wonderment. The sweet mixture of pine and sage filled the air. Trees lining the highway cast long shadows across the pavement, and sparse clouds intermittently filtered the sun as it crept higher into the morning sky.

Although I had read about it extensively, this was my first visit to Yellowstone Park. We had just entered the largest active volcano in the world, but that thought was far from my mind, lost in the grand scenery of dark green conifer-clad mountains and crystal clear streams.

Unlike Mount Shasta in Northern California, Yellowstone's volcano doesn't fit the common perception of a volcano as a cone-shaped mountain created from accumulated magma. Instead of building a mountain, a catastrophic explosion like those that have occurred at Yellowstone leaves a vast caldera (a geological depression created from the explosion of a volcano). Even though it was obvious to geologists that Yellowstone must be that sort of volcano, they didn't discover the caldera until the 1960s.

According to Bill Bryson in *A Short History of Nearly Everything*, at that time, NASA was busy testing some new high-altitude cameras by taking pictures of Yellowstone. Fortuitously, someone thought that the photos would make a nice display at the visitor center and sent some of them to park officials. From those pictures, Bryson explains, the park officials discovered the caldera and determined that it was approximately forty miles across—some 2.2 million acres, much too large to be recognizable as a caldera from the ground.

Scientists have since determined that Yellowstone is a supervolcano that sits atop an enormous reservoir of molten rock originating at least 125 miles inside the earth. The chamber of magma that fuels the myriad vents, geysers, mud pots, and hot springs is roughly the same distance across as the caldera, about 45 miles.

According to seismologists, who make a living studying these things, cataclysmic eruptions like the one that formed the park occur only after long intervals of about six hundred to eight hundred thousand years. The last eruption, which scientists believe to have been a thousand times more powerful than that of Mount St. Helens in 1980, left ash over a vast area that now encompasses nineteen Western states, as well as parts of Canada and Mexico. These same scientists believe that the Yellowstone volcano will erupt again just as it did some six hundred forty thousand years ago. If they're correct, it may be a cataclysmic event of biblical proportions. If by some remote chance, the volcano blows while I'm there, I can think of far less enjoyable things to be doing during the last moments of my life than fishing Yellowstone.

If there's a downside to Yellowstone, it's having to deal with the restrictions that park officials have placed on the three million people who visit each year during the three months that the park is open. Allowing three million visitors unfettered access to the park would soon destroy the many environmentally delicate areas, but the protective measures can be frustrating. The roads are narrow and winding, often by design, to keep the wheeled and foot traffic concentrated where officials want them. Consequently, traffic moves slowly, sometimes coming to a standstill.

We encountered a mild traffic jam on our way to Mammoth Hot Springs where we needed to buy a license to fish within the park boundaries. A mother black bear with her two bumbling cubs had just crossed the road, the cubs barely off the right shoulder, and cars were stopping in both directions. As car doors flew open and eager tourists jumped out to take a picture, Mama Bear looked back at her cubs as if to say, "Get your butts over here before one of those idiots does something stupid."

Yellowstone is an environment of paradoxes in which the modern and domestic coexist with the ancient and wild. Youthful tourists with cameras rush to capture their encounter with wild animals or the remnants of ancient cataclysms that helped to shape the continent. I wonder how many visitors to Yellowstone grasp its real significance. But even if all they remember are the geysers, mud pots, and bears, if those memories instill in them an ecological awareness and an interest in preserving important ecosystems, maybe the traffic jams are a small price to pay.

After Lex took a few pictures of the bears without getting out of the cab, I attempted to maneuver the pickup through the cars, most of which were parked half on the shoulder, leaving just enough room to squeeze by. The going was slow—I never knew when a kid might suddenly decide to jump out of a car—but easy enough until we encountered cars with open doors. Most of the people offered an obsequious smile and a conciliatory hand wave as they turned back to the car and shut the door. We would wave back and holler, "Thaaaaanks," in that long, drawn-out way that's a euphemism for "just get the hell out of the way."

Fortunately, the impatience of my youth had waned, and the beauty of the landscape sufficiently captured my attention to keep me from wanting to strangle the shit out of a bunch of tourists. Of course, if someone had hollered for the damn tourists to get out of the way, they could just as easily been talking to me since I was a tourist, too. At any rate, I was too excited about getting on the river to let some slow-me-to-death sons of bitches ruin my day. Well, maybe the impatience of my youth hadn't waned all that much. Still, I was glad to be there.

The main geological attraction at Mammoth Hot Springs is the travertine (a type of limestone deposited by hot springs) terraces. As we began our descent through the switchbacks from the ridge above Mammoth, the vegetation decreased. With little soil and abundant calcium deposits covering the ground, trees and other plants struggled to survive.

When we reached the headquarters at Mammoth, the store, restaurant, and restrooms were alive with tourists. Not being big on crowds and wanting to get to the river, we decided not to linger.

With the necessary fishing license paperwork completed and our fees paid, we turned and headed for the front door just as a young man of sixteen or seventeen was coming in. He had shoulder-length dark hair that probably hadn't seen a comb that day, an early indication of a c'est la vie approach to life. Déjà vu engulfed me as memories of my own youth came rushing back. Then the sound of my youngest daughter, Erin's, voice flashed through my mind, interrupting my thoughts with "Bed head ahead!"

My eyes moved from the mop with a neck for a handle to the T-shirt he was wearing, with the phrase "Pine Inch Nenis" blazoned across the front. It took only a split-second for my mind to rearrange the letters.

Lex and I both erupted in hysterical laughter and had to grab our knees for support.

We were nearly oblivious to the stares as some people stepped back apprehensively and others moved from behind aisle shelves or peered around them to catch a better look at the crazy bastards.

As I straightened up to catch my breath, my abdominal muscles hurt, and my laughter dwindled to a chortle.

The kid looked at me with mild bewilderment and said, "What's so funny, dude?"

"Kitschy shirt, man!" I said.

He looked perplexed, so I assumed that he was unsure whether my statement was a compliment. I initially thought he was searching the recesses of his mind for a definition of *kitschy,* but when he glanced down at his shirt, I realized that he was trying to remember which shirt he was wearing. Judging by its crumpled, slept-in appearance, putting on the shirt was a distant memory, and if he was anything like me at that age, he'd forgotten most of what he'd done yesterday.

He looked up with a carefree smirk, nodding like a bobblehead doll. I extended my arm for one of those closed-fist handshakes. He raised his arm, our knuckles met briefly, and he walked by. I still don't think he knew what *kitschy* meant, nor did he care. Apparently for him, as for kids in the 70s, anything that the establishment considered cheesy and tasteless was cool. What's cool about getting older is that you can be a smartass with an expanded vocabulary.

An attractive, sandy-haired woman in her mid-thirties looked at the boy's shirt as he passed. With a confused expression, she cocked her head like the dog in the RCA commercial, then turned quizzically and looked at a man I assumed was her husband. He was laughing, too, and after chuckling a few seconds longer, he leaned over and whispered in her ear. Her jaw dropped, her brow raised, and her eyes widened as she snapped a look at her husband. Then she began to smile.

Her look instantly turned from amusement to embarrassment when our eyes met and she realized that I had been watching. Her face turned as red as a Bing cherry, and she whirled around and headed on the long trot for the back corner of the store. The man looked at me with a prideful, Cheshire cat grin, winked, and turned to follow her.

As we headed for the front door, I said to Lex, "Ever notice how today's teenagers look and even act like the ones we grew up with in the early seventies? It's a little unsettling."

"That kid with the T-shirt reminds me of—well, me," replied Lex.

"Some people said we had an independent, anti-authority, don't-give-a-shit attitude," I reminisced as we descended the steps of the store.

"I'm pretty sure you did," replied Lex. "Hell, I think you still do about half the time."

"I just don't like dealing with dumb asses," I said. "Of course, I'm still hanging out with you, so I'm not completely intolerant."

"I may be the only one on the planet that will put up with your weak bullshit," retorted Lex.

"Make that two," I replied. My wife would be the other, but don't ask me to explain why.

We arrived at the Blacktail Deer Creek trailhead a little after

9:00 a.m. Cotton-ball clouds began to appear in the western sky and the air was warming rapidly, a recipe for an afternoon thunderstorm. "Could be a nice PMD hatch this morning," Lex said. Pale morning duns are mayflies of the genus *Ephemerella*. They hatch all summer, and the nymphs (immature insects) emerge into duns (early adult stage but not sexually mature) during the day between midmorning and midafternoon, sometimes earlier or later on especially warm days.

"It's getting warm," I said, lowering the tailgate of the pickup. "We'd better get started."

We grabbed our backpacks that held our waders, boots, rain jackets, fishing vests, reels and the tubes that housed our fly rods.

We each had one five- and one six-weight rod in our packs in case one rod got broken. It was more than three miles to the river, and if you break a rod and have to hike back to the pickup your fishing day is essentially over. Being angry because you broke a rod is one thing, but not longer being able to fish because you broke your only rod is a different level of unhappiness.

We checked to make sure that we had all the necessary fly boxes and then added our sandwiches and water bottles to the rest of the gear in our packs. Shouldering our packs, we started down the trail to the river.

Sweet, pungent sage soon replaced the fresh scent of pine at the trailhead as we followed the winding trail through open sagebrush country to the river, about an hour's hike. Fortunately, the four-letter word in fly-fishing, *wind,* was nonexistent.

Since that first day on Rock Creek, I had spent many pleasurable hours studying fly-fishing. I had a great deal of information crammed into my head, much of which I had yet put into practice.

One thing I understood clearly was that fly-fishing is both an art and a science. The art of fly-fishing involves skill: casting technique and the ability to place your fly at a precise spot. The science, in contrast, involves knowledge: the type of fly you offer and where you place it in, or on, the water. Successful fly-fishing combines the developed art of casting and line positioning with the applied sciences of hydrology, aquatic entomology, and ichthyology. Although a basic understanding of at least some scientific principles is helpful, you won't need a college degree or course in Latin to wade through the science of fly-fishing. Of course, you'll occasionally run into the boorish fly fisher who can, and all too often does, attempt to impress you with his knowledge of the Latin terms for the insects that trout eat.

Knowing that mayflies fall into the order of Ephemeroptera, of which there are many families, numerous genera, and myriad species, does little to help you catch fish. It's less important to know that a pale morning dun could be an *Ephemerella inermis* or an *Ephemerella infrequens* than it is to know that it's a light-colored mayfly more often than not successfully imitated with gray or cream-colored mayfly pattern—a fly designed and tied to represent an insect— like the Adams or Light Cahill dry fly. In other words, you need to know which insect the trout are eating at a particular place and time, which stage of metamorphosis the insect is in, and which fly to use to imitate that insect.

We heard the water before we saw it. Intermittent whispers of water splashing over the rocks became increasingly louder as we neared the river, and soon we began catching glimpses of the turbulent white water of small rapids through the sparse lodgepole pine along the river. As we descended the slope and followed the bank upstream, the clear, bluish hue of the flat water appeared in full view. We stopped at the edge of the water to enjoy the picturesque panorama along the far bank.

We found a little, open flat near the bank and removed our

packs to string up our rods. I hadn't noticed the sweat under my pack until that moment. In the shade of the trees, my shirt felt cool as the dry air evaporated the dampness. I sat for a few minutes drinking some water while Lex put on his waders and rigged up.

"What are you tying on?" I asked.

"An Adams and a Hare's Ear dropper," he replied. A dropper is a second fly tied to trail behind the first one.

I pulled my waders from my pack and put them on. I was just pulling my rod from the tube when Lex turned and said, "I'll give 'em a go," and started up the river.

I liked Lex's choice of flies and was inclined to try the same, but since we like to fish different bugs until we're sure what works best, I tied on an Elk Hair Caddis dry fly and a Pheasant Tail nymph as a dropper. Then I donned my pack and began fishing the stretch of water that Lex had bypassed and left for me.

Every now and then, a pale morning dun would emerge in the blue-green water and ride the current, its wings standing straight up like tiny sails. Soon afterward, with its wings sufficiently dried, it would gently flutter, lift off, and disappear into the foliage. No fish were rising.

After about thirty minutes, I reached the point in the river where Lex had started. It looked like the Caddis wouldn't raise a fish that morning, so I reeled up and headed upstream to see how Lex was getting along.

I found him intently working the lower part of a long, deep-water bend. The sight of numerous dimples regularly appearing on the flat surface just a few yards upstream from him stopped me in my tracks. I hadn't seen any serious bug activity to entice this kind of feeding behavior where I'd been fishing downriver. Obviously, something was going on up there in the tail of that channel run, so

I hastened my pace.

The rising fish—a half dozen or so big cutthroat trout—were leaving distinct rings as they gently surfaced and submerged in one smooth motion, like porpoises in a calm bay that seem in no particular hurry to go anywhere. My excitement grew as I got closer but tempered as I watched Lex making drift after drift to no avail.

"What are they feeding on?" I asked.

"Damned if I know!" he exclaimed. "Shit, one of them took something not six inches from my Adams. They haven't even looked at it."

"Maybe they'll eat a lighter-colored PMD," I said as I clipped off the Elk Hair Caddis and Pheasant Tail and placed them on the small square of sheepskin on my vest. "I saw a few coming off the water downstream."

"I saw a few, too, but the trout aren't interested in the Adams," he said.

"Nice fish, eh?" I prodded, looking up from tying on my fly.

"Ya think?" Lex shot back. "They're big bastards!"

"Well, they don't get big by being stupid," I said. "Let's see if they'll eat a Comparadun." A Comparadun is a dry fly tied to make it float low in the water.

"Build to 'em!" Lex said as I walked up near where he was standing. It's a phrase ropers use when they're building a loop—making the loop larger—while they're hotly pursuing a calf or steer.

These are big bastards! I thought as I peeled some line off my reel. Many of these fish looked longer than eighteen inches, every bit as big as some of the rainbows we'd caught the previous spring on the Big Horn.

My expectations were running amuck as I prepared to cast. For a moment, I thought I was actually dreaming.

I set my sights on one fish that was consistently surfacing in almost rhythmic fashion and decided to cast to him. Even though my drifting ability didn't yet equal Lex's, it had advanced sufficiently to fool most fish.

After making several drifts directly over the top of this particular fish, I began to realize that we weren't dealing with "most" fish. Our fly lines weren't spooking the fish and sending them down to the bottom. It wasn't so much that they were oblivious to our presence; they just didn't seem to give a shit.

Lex had just finished tying on a new fly, and I could tell that he was eager to get back into the action.

"What did you tie on?" I asked.

"PMD emerger," he replied, meaning an emerging nymph about to hatch into an adult. "They've got to be eating something in the surface film."

I made a few more unsuccessful drifts. "Here, get back in the fight, son," I said as I stepped to the bank to figure out what to try next. I waited to see if Lex's emerger worked before deciding.

Lex stepped to the edge of the water, gracefully built a sufficient amount of line in two false casts, and then gently rolled out a perfect cast that landed about ten feet upstream from a rising fish. Lex was crouched, gently pulling slack as he followed the fly with the tip of his rod. He leaned forward, gradually tensing, ready to set the hook as the fly entered the zone where the fish had been rising.

The fly was drifting perfectly toward where the fish had surfaced. In a few more feet, opportunity and skill would meet in a triumphant climax; the take would come. I had been standing motionless since the fly hit the water, but now I began to tense, bending sideways at the waist as if I were trying to coax the eight ball into the side pocket to win the game. *Here it comes.*

Just as the fly passed, the fish surfaced leisurely in nearly the same location as before, seemingly unaware of the emerger's presence. Realizing that there would be no take, I slowly straightened up and watched the fly reach the end of its drift.

As the line straightened and the fly began to create a V-shaped wake, Lex straightened up with a look of bewilderment. His hands dropped to his sides. Looking at me over the top of his glasses, he said, "What the hell does a guy need to do?"

Fly-fishing has a way of tempering egos, especially with a little prodding from your fishing partner. It's our duty, a requirement, really, to make sure that our fishing friends' egos remain in check. Believe me, if I were in his place, I would be catching hell.

Remember Rock Creek, I thought as if Rock Creek were the Alamo.

"That fish made you look like Ned in the first reader," I chided. "You know, like Dick and Jane's dim-witted cousin."

He shot me half a peace sign and then picked up his rod. More determined than ever, he launched another cast out over the water. After a quick mend (a flip of the rod to position his line so as not to drag the fly on the surface unnaturally), the fly drifted to almost the same place as the last one. The fish rolled well ahead of the fly and, just as the fly passed, gave a little flick of his tail as his dorsal fin submerged, splashing water about two feet in Lex's direction.

"Did you see that?" I shouted to get Lex's attention

"What?" Lex replied, startled.

"That fish just flipped you off," I retorted.

"Piss on you," he shot back.

"That fish has no respect for you at all," I added. "Hell, I'm beginning to lose a little respect for you too, oh, great white fisherman."

Referring to Lex as white is an understatement. His Irish ancestry shows in his red hair and very pale skin. If it weren't for the freckles on his legs, they would be completely fluorescent. On the few occasions during the summer when it's so hot that Lex dons a pair of shorts, anyone standing within fifty yards of him needs to wear polarized sunglasses, the darker, the better. The first time I saw his legs, I thought he was wearing a pair of angora chaps and threatened to bring welding goggles next time to protect me from the snowlike glare.

"I can't believe these sons-a-bitches," he shouted.

Visions of John McEnroe pissing on the judge's leg in a fit of rage over a line call flashed into my mind. Lex's Irish was up, making him even more determined to catch a fish but also myopic in his thought process. He picked up his line and flipped it back upstream.

My awe at the size of these fish and their seeming indifference to our offerings turned to inquisition. Something about the porpoise like rises gnawed at me. Synapses fired in my brain, trying to bridge some connections to relevant information archived in the subterranean recesses of my mind. It was like knocking on a door that I was expecting myself to answer and not being able to find the knob.

In his fascinating book, *Changing Minds*, Howard Gardner wrote, "[G]ut feelings do not arise fully formed, like Athena from the head of Zeus, [but] represent a partially conscious but difficult-to-articulate recognition of the resemblance of a present situation to earlier ones, where one course of action proved far superior to its rivals." My gut was telling me that this was a recognizable situation, but it was not yet a fully formed instinct.

The essence of instinct is our ability to resurrect information instantaneously. I had read about rise forms, which are the various ways trout break the water's surface when they're feeding, but I had too little experience relating them to the range of associated situations to recognize the meaning of this one, let alone articulate it.

About twenty different rise forms are recognized and cataloged in various publications and articles, all of which, obviously, tell us that trout are feeding on or near the surface. However, only a few of these rise forms tell us anything important. A select few indicate which insect the fish are feeding on and/or the stage of their life cycle. These rise forms are, of course, the important ones, and I was sure that this porpoising rise form was one of them.

The rise form I did remember, having spent many great days fishing spring creeks near home where caddis flies are abundant, was the "slash." Trout seem to know that if they intend to eat a caddisfly, they had better catch him before he gets to the surface because he won't be there long. Caddisfly pupae move to the surface rapidly enough to break through the surface film easily and take off quickly as adults. Consequently, trout chase the pupae to the surface, catching them either before or as they reach the surface. The trout's momentum carries him to the surface where, often with his quarry firmly secured, he turns abruptly, making a splashy exit, and heads back to safer depths, creating a slash in the water as he swims.

The methodical porpoising, in contrast to the "slash," obviously represented trout in no great hurry. We had noticed bugs lifting off the surface earlier, but there were few if any now, and yet at least a half a dozen trout were surfacing. Lex was busy making some of the prettiest drifts I had ever seen, cussing every time his fly passed over a spot where a trout had previously risen. He was like a sage in my mind, and I might have begun seriously questioning that status if I hadn't been so busy playing the aquatic invertebrate version of Trivial Pursuit.

The sun was behind one of the many scattered clouds, casting a shadow and leaving little light to help contrast any floating bugs with the water below them. Standing in mid-calf-deep water, I bent over for a closer look. As my head got close enough to see any small insects floating on or near the surface, the fishing net attached to a loop on the back of my vest's collar flopped over my shoulder. As I grabbed it to toss it back, it dawned on me that the fine, soft, synthetic mesh of my catch-and-release net might make a great seine.

I detached the net using the quick-release clip and waded out into thigh-deep water about ten yards below the rising fish. Lex continued to drift his PMD emerger without as much as a look from the fish. His usually white, freckled face had taken on a reddish hue from obvious frustration.

I placed the net in the bluish-green water and began to move it across the flow to seine the surface to a depth of eight or so inches. After about fifteen seconds, I waded back to ankle-deep water, crouched down, flipped down the magnifying glasses clipped to my cap, and turned the net inside out, lifting it closer to the glasses to bring anything on the surface into focus.

"I'll be damned!" I exclaimed loudly as the rise form article I'd read came rushing back to me. "Fucking spinners," I whispered. Spinners (mayflies in the sexually mature, late-adult stage) fall spent onto the water after mating. *That's why these trout are in no hurry,* I thought. *The bugs are dead.*

"What—?" Lex asked. "What the hell is it?"

"Let me see your fly," I commanded.

He let his drift continue further downstream and then flipped it closer to me where I could reach it as he stepped to the bank. I clipped off his emerger and pulled a fly out of the box I had just retrieved from my vest pocket.

"What are you putting on?" Lex inquired as he walked up to me.

"Take a look," I said, handing him the net.

He pulled the net close. "What kind of mayflies are these?"

"Dead ones," I replied, "and most are partially submerged. There must have been a hell of a spinner fall somewhere upstream earlier this morning." That explained the unhurried porpoising; those bugs weren't going anywhere, and the fish knew it.

As I tied the size 14 Rusty Spinner dry fly (designed to imitate a dead adult mayfly) onto Lex's leader, I added excitedly, "I read about almost this exact situation in a magazine article." I pulled the clinch knot tight, clipped the loose tag end, pinched the barb on the hook, and then put some floatant on the leader beginning about six inches above the fly. "Don't worry about it sinking," I directed. "Just keep your eye on the floating leader if you can see it. If you see a rise near where you think the fly is, set the hook."

Lex walked back to where he'd been casting before and made a nice cast that floated out over the water and then a crisp mend followed by what looked like the beginning of a drag-free drift. The fly entered the zone. The dorsal fin of what looked like a nice cutthroat broke the surface, and the leader straightened.

Lex lifted the rod and hollered, "I got him, son!"

Lex's playing that trout was a thing of beauty. The fish made some short runs and then tried to hang near the bottom, but Lex wasn't having any of that and turned the fish sideways to the current, making him move. This tactic seemed to aggravate the fish further, and he came to the surface, rolled and flopped in a tantrum, and began slapping the leader with his tail. Lex finally got the fish's head up and guided him into my waiting net about twenty feet downstream.

Lex slogged down to take a closer look as I held, through the soft, black mesh of the net, the biggest cutthroat I had ever seen, let alone touched. The hen was about twenty-two inches long and beautiful almost beyond description, her head and back a grayish olive with a few black spots around her head that increased to abundance around her tail as if someone had been too liberal with a peppershaker. Her gill plates were a pinkish red, and she had a narrow band of faded pink running the length of her deep, firm side. A blaze of orange adorned the pleated underside of her lower jaw as if her throat had, in fact, been cut.

Solidly built and thick around the middle, she felt cool and heavy like a wet bag of lead shot when I picked her up to remove the hook. She had taken the rusty spinner without hesitation. It was deep in her cotton-white mouth. I grabbed my small forceps, carefully reached in, and grasped the fly. Even as deep as it was, the barbless hook came out with only the slightest twist.

"Get your camera, and I'll get a picture of you with your fish," I instructed.

Lex quickly laid his rod on the bank, ran up to his camouflaged pack, and began digging for the camera.

I kept the fish submerged in the net so she could breathe while Lex returned with the camera. After trading the net for the camera, I took a nice picture of Lex crouching in the water holding the fish through the net, which he held just above the water.

"Got it," I said.

Lex placed her in about twelve inches of water, gently cradling her with both hands under her belly, and we watched her slowly swim away in the clear, blue-green water.

"Incredible," Lex exclaimed.

"Nice cutthroat!" I said, extending my hand.

"Thanks," he replied as he shook it.

A sense of accomplishment engulfed me, the kind a guide must feel when he puts you on a good fish. I had actually applied what I had read to a real-life fishing situation and helped a friend hook the largest cutthroat trout he had ever caught and I had ever seen.

The vision of that beautiful fish burned into my consciousness, a milestone on the path of my increasing competence.

Chapter 3

Winter Blues

There aren't many places in Minnesota, my current home, where fly fishers can get their winter fix and shake off what John Gierach in *Another Lousy Day in Paradise* refers to as the "shack nasties." For most other anglers, the treatment for cabin fever is a trip to a nearby frozen lake and several hours of staring into a hole in the ice pursuing the lethargic fish that lurk in the dark water below.

According to the Minnesota Department of Natural Resources website, ice fishing is "a true Minnesota adventure." I agree. But then, after you've been cooped up in the house for several sunless, windy, subzero days, just about any outdoor activity seems like an adventure. Walking out to the county road to get the paper is an adventure.

Ice fishing is as good an excuse as any to get out of the house, I suppose. Any change of venue is a welcome relief, especially for the sake of sport. Cultural anthropologists suggest that consorting outdoors, defying the elements to pursue an elusive quarry, is a natural, instinctual male behavior, a remnant of our hunter-gatherer ancestry.

The list of activities (or excuses for getting out of the house) that men can rationalize with this explanation is virtually endless. Once, when I pointed out to my wife that we can't help it—fishing and hunting is a man thing—she kept demanding an explanation, so I simply asked her to explain what motivates her endless hours of shopping. Of course, it was a rhetorical question. I wasn't looking for an answer; I just wanted Bert—my affectionate nickname for her—to recognize the analogy. Well, maybe I was trying to stir her up a little.

After a few minutes of further questioning and genteel debate, Bert said with a wry smile and a noticeable degree of finality, "We can't help it. Shopping's like gathering berries; it's a woman thing." Using my own logic against me, damn it; I hate it when that happens. If your wife reacts more explosively than mine to this line of questioning, you have an immediate and vividly apparent reason to go fishing: saving your marriage.

Ice-fishing comforts may be as simple as a five-gallon bucket to sit on; top-of-the-line models have a seat-cushion lid and some are camouflaged for use during hunting season. Of course, a bucket provides the added benefit of being a place to keep your favorite beverage and other trappings.

Buckets are popular early in the season when the temperature is still above zero. By the time the ice is thick enough to drive on (it's never thick enough for me!), the icehouses start appearing.

Icehouses can be as simple as a tentlike structure on a plastic sled that you can drag out onto the lake, but when the ice is thick enough to support the weight of an SUV, the accommodations become more elaborate. Insulated, generator-powered ice cabins featuring propane space heaters, bunks, and televisions—wouldn't want to miss the Vikings game—arrive on utility trailers and turn a portion of the lake into what looks suspiciously like a neighborhood in the movie *Grumpy Old Men*.

Occasionally, when the ice melts early, some icehouses end up as condos for the walleye, northern pike, and perch, the miniature versions of which you can find in home aquariums.

The one problem ice fishers never encounter is keeping their beer cold—just the opposite, in fact. When the mercury drops to near zero, keeping your beer from freezing is the challenge. In theory, you use the same ice chest you used last summer to keep beer cold to prevent your beer from freezing. In reality, subzero temperatures will eventually invade the ice chest and wreak havoc on most beverages. Last spring, in the garage, I found half a dozen beer cans in an ice chest I had forgotten to clean out, with their sides split open.

Beginning in November, billboards along the highways advertise whiskey with a tagline that goes something like, ". . . because you don't have to worry about it freezing." Whiskey's low freezing point partially explains the seasonality of my scotch consumption and liquor sales in general. Of course, the short daylight—barely eight hours at the winter solstice—and frequent overcast days may also have something to do with the popularity of hard liquor in winter.

Whiskey, of course, is just one way of cheering ourselves up during the coldest months. But even with roaring fires, winter sports, and festive holidays, many people still suffer from gloom and depression in winter. Researchers have even discovered a diagnosable medical condition, Seasonal Affective Disorder (SAD), which they believe is caused by sunlight deprivation. Dr. Norman Rosenthal, a pioneer in SAD research, used the term "winter blues" to describe a mild form of this disorder in the title of his first publication on the subject, *Winter Blues: Everything You Need to Know to Beat Seasonal Affective Disorder.*

Although the blue feeling most often affects people who live at latitudes above fifty degrees in either hemisphere, according to Dr. Rosenthal, it can also affect people in lower latitudes to a lesser degree. It occurs even in Florida. It's hard for those of us who live in Minnesota to understand how people in Florida could suffer from

SAD. We go to Florida for treatment. Where the hell do they go?

A *New York Times* article I read recently states that those who suffer "declines in energy, cheerfulness, creativity, or productivity" during the dark days of winter can usually find relief through exercise and increased outdoor activity, particularly on sunny days. Nothing against ice fishing, mind you, but sitting on your butt all day inside a shack looking at your ice hole, is certainly not exercise or an outdoor activity, sun or no sun. Still, given the symptoms of SAD noted in the *New York Times* article, no one wants your sorry butt hanging around the house, so go fishing. Even ice fishing is better than doing nothing and driving your wife crazy.

Two other SAD symptoms are worth noting. According to the experts, an appetite for carbohydrates, including those found in alcohol, replaces sex drive for SAD sufferers. It's just as well that you have less interest in sex, considering that with your attitude during this period, you're not likely to get any, anyway. The up side is that you now have a legitimate, scientific rationale for craving alcohol, at least in the winter: it's a carbohydrate thing. I tried to explain this reasoning to my wife. "Hon, this craving for alcohol in winter has been well researched by medical professionals," I said, wearing my best poker face.

"Oh, great," Bert retorted with more than a hint of sarcasm. "A medical excuse for hanging out with your buddies all day, swilling beer? You assholes are in this together." Maybe we are, but that's my story and I'm sticking to it.

After several cloudy, subzero days in a row, during which I looked on mundane tasks that involved venturing outside, like taking out the trash or getting the mail, as monumental endeavors, the weatherman predicted clearing skies and rising temperatures. Obviously tired of my sulking, my wife recommended that I go to the river the next day and "shake the stink off" with some fly-fishing. She didn't need to tell me twice.

One of the advantages of midwinter fly-fishing is that you don't need to get on the water early in the morning. The insects aren't very active (so the fish aren't feeding aggressively) until the sun gets on the water, so getting to the river before ten o'clock is unnecessary. The drive to the Whitewater River is about two-and-a-half hours, so after packing a lunch and a couple of beers and filling a thermos with coffee, I left the house a little after seven o'clock for some much needed seasonal therapy.

With the thermos full of hot coffee and the gear packed neatly in the backseat of my extended-cab Chevy pickup, I pulled out onto the highway just as the sun was breaking through a thin layer of leftover clouds on the horizon, the refracted light creating a bright orange glow. At that time of year, the sun remains low in the southern sky, so I was driving into the sunlight for most of the trip. I wasn't complaining, though. After several days with no sun, I was happy to put on my sunglasses and drive with my visor down. I felt like the king of the road as I tooled down the highway, sipping coffee and listening to National Public Radio. *What a great day to be on the river,* I thought.

The gently rolling farmland south of the Twin Cities along Highway 52, my route to the Whitewater River, is some of the most productive soil in the upper Midwest. The deep, dark earth is ideal for the two dominant crops: corn and soybeans. During the growing season, the occasional pasture or hayfield contributes to a mosaic of varying green tones that looks from the air like a patchwork quilt. Now, dead grass, bare fields, and leafless, gray trees dominated the landscape, and snow, which appeared a little deeper than at home, hid those fields and pastures from my view.

Driving through Rochester, the largest town in the area and home to the famous Mayo Clinic, I noticed that the time and temperature on one of the bank signs read 9:06 and 31 degrees, respectively. *Should be on the river by ten o'clock,* I thought. Between the coffee and the anticipation, I was getting a little antsy about getting on the water. I rolled my shoulders; the tension subsided, and the winter blues began to fade.

East of Rochester the terrain becomes steeper as you enter the Driftless Area. A large Karst region—a limestone region containing caves and underground streams—the Driftless Area comprises about twenty thousand square miles in western Wisconsin, northeastern Iowa, southeastern Minnesota, and extreme northwestern Illinois. Unable to locate moraine (rock debris left on the surface after glaciers retreat), geologists concluded that continental glaciers had not drifted over the area, hence the term "driftless." The undisturbed Paleozoic era bedrock became subject to erosion when the glaciers retreated, leaving the region with numerous spring-fed creeks that feed the Mississippi River. Interestingly, French explorers and early settlers called this region Coulee, based on the French word *couler,* meaning, "to flow."

Bordered by picturesque tree-lined bluffs, the Mississippi River and its spring creek tributaries offer dramatic scenery and provide a winter home to countless bald eagles. Many of the spring creeks in the Driftless Area are cool enough to support a year-round, naturally reproducing trout population.

Less than an hour after leaving Rochester, I entered the Whitewater State Park. I was so intent looking at the river, which runs right along the highway, that I left a nose print on the driver's side window. I cuss the dog for doing that.

I pulled into the park headquarters a little before ten o'clock. Even though they'd been plowed, the entrance and road to the park office remained covered with an inch or so of packed snow that crunched loudly as I drove over it. The river was about fifty yards behind the office. Driving slowly, I strained to catch glimpses of it.

The park office was open, and since this was my first visit to the park, I went in to gather information that might save me some time and effort, such as where to park and which section of the river has the most productive water. Other than the park ranger and the cheerful woman who managed the office, it looked as though I had the park to myself. Since the river runs right through the middle of the park and is only sixty yards or so from the campground parking lot, it's not the place to fish during the regular season. It's too accessible, and, once school lets out for the summer, the campers are as thick as fleas on a stray cat. However, between January and March, Whitewater State Park is a great place for quiet solitude and a few nice fish.

The Whitewater River is a classic spring creek, a type of free-flowing stream so called because it's fed by springs. Except during the spring runoff of melted snow or periodic heavy rains, spring creeks have consistent flows of very pure, clean water. Many springs in southeastern Minnesota maintain a water temperature between fifty and sixty degrees year round. Streams fed by a sufficient number of these springs, including the Whitewater, maintain a consistent temperature over long distances regardless of the season or weather, making them an excellent habitat for trout.

Because the water temperature remains well above freezing during the winter months, enabling these streams to support plant life, the insect population that feeds on the plants thrives and remains active throughout the winter, providing food for the trout. A consistent water temperature helps keep the fish nearly as active in January as in June. The short winter days may limit that activity to four or five hours, but that small window can provide for some active and productive fly-fishing.

I researched the area earlier that winter and found out that the springs feeding the streams originate from aquifers made up of layers of sand, gravel, and broken rock consisting primarily of limestone, a sedimentary rock composed largely of calcite or calcium carbonate, mostly from the exoskeletons of marine organisms from ancient seas. Because this form of calcium is water-soluble, the springs consistently maintain a pH in the stream of more than 7.5, ideal for a variety of insects and trout.

This consistent aquatic environment produces fish that are very particular in their choice of food, requiring that you closely match the size and color of the currently active local insects if you want to catch any fish.

During the year, you have literally hundreds of flies to choose from. With a little experience, you can whittle these choices down to a select few by season, time of day, and weather conditions. When you're new to fly-fishing or even to a particular stream, choosing the right fly can be a cumbersome, frustrating process of trial and error, but experienced fly fishers or those who have done a little homework enjoy this kind of challenge. In the winter the choices are midges and small dark stoneflies.

I like having to figure out what the fish will take. Often, the first thing I do before I rig up is walk out into the stream and pick up a few rocks in the current to see what kind of bugs are present, particularly noting their size and color. Of course, it helps if you know what you're looking at. One of the first and, frankly, one of the handiest, books I have used is *Hatch Guide for Western Streams* by Jim Schollmeyer. Despite the title, the book applies to more than just western streams, and it covers many of the insect species that inhabit most of the North American cold-water streams important to fly fishers. This book remains in my travel bag, and I regularly refer to it when I'm fishing.

After parking near the deserted campground, I decided to walk down to the river and look. The water was perfectly clear, literally glistening from the fast, shallow riffle water made choppy by a heavily cobbled river bottom. The riffle fed a narrow, deep run of fast-flowing water in the center with slower current in the margins. The sun behind me warmed the back of my neck as I stepped to the edge of the water, its light illuminating the bottom. I spent a few minutes scanning the slower, smoother water in the tail of a run where I noticed a couple of twelve-inch trout on the far side delicately nosing sand that had accumulated behind a large rock, possibly trying to locate midge larvae or a burrower-type nymph. This kind of feeding activity indicated that the bugs weren't active, but with warming temperatures, that could quickly change. Then, I looked into the faster water near the center of the stream looking for long, dark shapes parallel to the flow or the flashing that indicates trout feeding on drifting bugs. Nothing. Not surprising, though, as it was still early.

As I turned to head back to the truck and put on my waders, I decided to use a midge larva pattern drifted on the bottom. Midge larvae (very tiny and worm-like) are the dominant food source for trout during the winter months on most rivers.

Choosing a midge might sound straightforward until you consider that over a thousand species in the family *Chironomidea* inhabit North America. The problem is not so much the number of species, since many midge species important as a food for trout act the same way, as the wide variety of colors they come in. In the absence of any experience with a particular body of water, the trial-and-error method is all you have. Black or red are the most common colors for midge larvae, so it's best to start there.

Considering that there was no wind and that only a little weight would be required to get the nymphs down to the stream bottom, I decided to string up my four-weight rod, a medium-action rod ideal for small nymphs as well as for dry flies.

As I sat on the tailgate of the pickup sipping the last of the coffee and rigging up, the sun shined as brightly as on any summer day, I could feel the energy returning. The apathetic, lethargic feeling that had overwhelmed me during the winter months was slowly being exorcised from my mind and body. Every breath of cold, clean, fresh outdoor air was invigorating, making me want to get up and do something, anything. *Let's make something happen,* I thought as I gulped down the last swallow of coffee and jumped down off the tailgate. Grabbing my rod, I started down the trail to the river with a determined rhythm. "Be afraid, fish. Be very afraid," I whispered.

The snow yielded softly and quietly under my feet as I made my way back to the stream, lost in the moment. I realized that in fly-fishing we seldom make something happen. We can only prepare ourselves for what might be and then let it happen. Often, we get our blinders on. Our determination is so intense that we miss many important things going on around us. Even in the best environment—a relatively warm, sunny, winter day alone on a beautiful spring creek when we're feeling so confident that we would take on a grizzly with a fly swatter—we can get lost in our own world, overlooking the signs that would likely take us where we want to go if we heeded them.

My appreciation of the glorious day faded and reality began to creep back in as I broke out of the trees into the twenty yards or so of clearing before the water's edge. This snow wasn't loud and crunchy like it had earlier when I first walked down and watched those two trout nosing the bottom.

I looked down at my wading boots, which were making relatively quiet footsteps in the snow. *It must be thirty-five degrees or so,* I thought as I looked up at the tail of the pool. *Shit!* I thought, as the rings of water from rising fish quickly appeared and then dissipated into the flow. "There's a full-blown midge hatch on."

A gut-knotting panic came over me as I tried to remember where my dry fly midge patterns were or whether I had even brought them.

Damn it! I thought as I scrambled through the pockets of my fishing vest. *Where the hell are they?*

Then I felt a wooden box, and it came back to me. I had recently reorganized my flies by placing the more likely useful patterns for this trip into my only wooden fly box. My gut relaxed a little. I took a deep breath and, with my lips pursed, exhaled noisily. *Be prepared and then just let it happen,* I thought.

I sat down on a streamside boulder, quickly removing the tiny split-shot weight and replacing the larva patterns with a size 20 black dry-fly imitation of an adult midge. Using my smooth-jawed forceps I flattened the barb on the dry fly to make removing the hook easier. With my fly box tucked into my vest pocket, I stood up and shook out some line with several false casts as I stepped into the first few inches of water.

There was a trout feeding in front of an exposed rock on the far side of the main flow. The rock was near the tail of the pool, creating a very small feeding lane. After a few additional false casts to gauge the distance, I cast across the center of the flow and dropped the fly about three feet in front of where the fish had surfaced. The trout came up and took a real midge about half a second before my fly reached her and had just dived back down as my fly passed over her. It was all I could do to resist the impulse to snap my rod up and re-present the fly to the same fish.

"Finish the drift" is a cardinal rule of fly-fishing, so I exhaled and continued to follow the fly with my rod tip. As I was taking up slack, my fly came around the rock and suddenly disappeared in a swirl.

Startled, I lifted the rod. The fish acted equally surprised and dashed behind the rock. The resistance from the rod caused it to change course, and head downstream. The trout hadn't come to the surface yet, but, as he entered the shallower water, I could see that he was a nice fish of maybe twelve or thirteen inches. I stepped down to the tail out (the shallow water at the end of the run) and pulled him to the surface for a closer look—a chunky little brown.

The nice thing about fishing with barbless hooks is the release. Many times, I just pitch the fish a little slack as he gets close and he unhooks himself with no handling. Even though this fish was only hooked on the lip, he couldn't shake the fly, so I pulled him up close, pinched the fly between my thumb and index finger, and gave a twist. In the blink of an eye, he was under that big rock again.

I inspected my fly, which was in decent shape but waterlogged. After applying some finely powdered desiccant to it, I stepped back to my original spot and began working on the first fish, which was still taking bugs in almost rhythmic fashion in front of the rock. I made several quality drifts, but the fish showed little interest.

Several fish were rising now in a number of locations upstream, but I wanted to work the closer fish first. Within a few minutes, another fish appeared closer to me, but I couldn't interest him in the black midge, either.

What bugs I had seen coming off the water looked lighter in color, so I pulled out the wooden fly box to see what else might work. I had a couple of size 22 Adamses, so I tied one on, thinking that the gray body might match the natural midges more closely. I wanted to take a shot at what appeared to be the bigger fish—a hen I thought— in front of the rock. I made the same cast as before, and when the fly reached the spot where she was surfacing, she sucked it in. I set the hook, and the fish immediately catapulted itself out of the water.

The dandy rainbow raced and jumped to every corner of the tail out, flipping and splashing water in all directions. She even made it upstream into the fast water of the run and then came rushing back down right at me. With the slack that she created, I thought she might shake the hook, but she didn't. I lifted my rod high, pulling her closer, and then gently slid my net under her. In the net was a silvery, fifteen-inch rainbow, a hint of pink running the length of her side. I noticed that the hook had come out of the fish while she was flopping in the net, so I stuck the net back in the water and turned it sideways.

What a lovely fish, I thought as she darted away.

That rainbow's antics had frightened every other fish in the lower run and tail out. Not one riser remained; the surface of the water was dead calm, not even a wrinkle.

By the time these fish get over that spooking, the hatch will likely be over, I surmised.

I spent the next three hours or so working my way upriver, using midge larvae and nymph patterns and thoroughly enjoying the afternoon. I hooked and landed several more trout of varying size in the seams of runs and other holding water. As the shadows grew longer in the narrowing canyon and the limestone outcroppings became more difficult to distinguish in the diminishing light, I realized that the fishing day was nearly over.

I headed back to the truck in the chill of the late afternoon, tired yet rejuvenated. The snow was crunchy again under my feet. As the sun moved lower in the sky, the temperature was dropping rapidly. My mouth began to water with a near-metallic sensation at the thought of the cold beer awaiting me in the truck.

I laid the rod across the bed rails of my truck and dropped the tailgate, unintentionally allowing it to hit the end of the support cables with a resounding thud. Sliding the red plastic ice chest out onto the gate, I grabbed a cold bottle of Shiner Bock.

Hearing the short, crisp hiss as I popped the top of that first beer, I realized that my winter blues had been set adrift sometime during the day like the initial vapor from the bottle. That first cold, tingling swallow was the prescribed medication topping off a five-hour treatment. I was cured of the winter blues but hopeful of a relapse.

Chapter 4

The High/Low Paradox

Whether 'tis nobler in the mind to ride the surface with a smartly dressed dry fly and nurture purist tradition or to embrace modern science with a perfectly dead-drifted nymph bounced along the streambed under the auspices of strike indicator methodology—that is the question.

In simpler terms, do I fish a dry fly or a nymph? Such seemingly small decisions can have monumental consequences. This fly-fishing is a tough business.

At times, this question is philosophical, allowing for spirited debate. More often, contemplating whether to "go high" with the dry fly or "go low" with the nymph is a straightforward question of which method is most likely to catch fish. Anglers who have caught thousands of fish in nearly every conceivable way on a fly rod may prefer the dry fly even when it's less likely to catch fish simply because it's the greater challenge. I'm not there yet.

***

It was a cool, overcast April day with a trace of snow in the air when we pulled out of the alley from behind the Cody, Wyoming, fly shop where Lex had just purchased a used drift boat. The sky blue inflatable boat had a matching blue patch in the bow where someone had run into a sharp stick and punctured her but was otherwise in great condition. The fly shop owner had ordered a new aluminum frame for the boat at Lex's request and had mounted it before we arrived. Headed for the Yellowstone River in Montana as the first stage of a six-day road trip, we were anxious to try the boat. Supposedly in search of trout, we were really in search of ourselves and of whatever was just over the hill.

That night, we stayed at Sam Phares's Ranch near Big Timber, Montana. The next morning was crisp, and the heavy frost made the boat look like a big, blue glazed doughnut. Even though the sun was shining when we left the ranch, it was still crisp, and the heater in Lex's pickup felt good. We bought a couple of coffees and breakfast sandwiches in Big Timber, hired a "shuttle" (person to drive the pickup and trailer from boat launch to the takeout downriver) at the local fly shop, and headed for the Greybull boat launch on the Yellowstone.

We officially launched Lex's "new" boat at 9:25 a.m. that bright April morning for what was to be her maiden voyage. Of course, she wasn't really a maiden, but she was a maiden to us, and, whether it's boats or women, that's all that really matters.

The fishing was a little slow, but we caught a few rainbows, the biggest about fourteen inches, all on nymphs. After that trip, we officially proclaimed her a river-worthy vessel and christened her, mostly because of her color, Ol' Blue. Her being a rubber raft made the traditional breaking of a bottle across the bow a difficult proposition, and, besides, we don't like wasting good alcohol, so we opened a bottle of Glenlivet scotch and simply toasted her sea-worthiness instead.

The next day, Lex and I pulled into the parking lot of the first boat launch below Ennis Lake on the lower Madison River in Montana. There were three or four cars in the parking lot but no anglers in sight. Our intent was to make the short four-and-a-half-mile float to Cherry Creek that afternoon.

A cool westerly breeze greeted us as we got out of the truck to walk down the boat launch and look at the river. Clouds like cotton balls drifted in tight formation overhead, allowing intermittent glimpses of cerulean sky. "Mostly cloudy," the meteorological types would call it. Creative bunch they are. Maybe that's why they majored in meteorology and not marketing.

We unloaded the boat and Lex began getting it ready while I drove the truck to the home of the woman who runs the shuttle service, a short distance from the Cherry Creek takeout where we would end our trip.

I pulled into her place, the empty trailer bouncing and clattering. As I got out of the pickup, several curious horses stared intently, their heads hanging over a slightly sagging net wire fence, ears perked forward, and three barking dogs trotted down the gravel driveway toward me. *Here comes the welcoming committee,* I thought.

I suppose you can never be a hundred percent sure how to read dogs in this situation, but if you deal with them often enough, you can get reasonably good at it. In general, I can read a bluffing dog, cow, or bull more easily than I can read a bluffing poker player. These dogs didn't look very tough, so when the woman didn't come out after a minute, I eased the door open, talking to the dogs in a confident, yet nonthreatening tone.

"Hey, big guy. How are you today?" I asked the closest one.

Their tails began to wag, so I bent down and slightly extended my hand, palm down. The shepherd, obviously the alpha male, came up and sniffed my hand. After that, the rest began squirming, nearly pissing all over themselves, and coming up to get their heads patted, too. Had I come to steal something, they probably would have shown me where it was.

As I stepped up on the front porch, the front door opened and a gray-haired woman about the same age as my mother stepped out, pulling her coat on. "Howdy!" she sang out as she extended her hand to shake mine.

"How are you, ma'am?" I asked.

"Fine." She replied.

By now, the rest of the dogs were all over Lex's truck tires, giving them a good sprinkling as if they had been saving up for days.

"You dogs get away from there!" she hollered with a good deal of authority. "Get back to the house, now!" Two of them headed to the house, but the big shepherd came up to her.

She patted him on the head, ordered him to stay, and then followed me in her SUV to the Cherry Creek takeout where I left the truck and boat trailer. On the way back upriver to the boat launch, she told me that she and her husband had built the place on the river and that he had passed away some time back.

"How long have you been running a shuttle?" I asked.

"About five years. Started it right after my husband passed." She said. "Just to make ends meet."

"Should be a good place to have a shuttle business," I said.

"Yes, but it's getting a little tougher with the price of fuel and the Bureau of Land Management raising my fees," She replied. "But all the local fly shops throw business my way, so I'm in good hands."

She pulled in near the boat launch; I paid her in cash and thanked her, and she drove away. By that time, Lex had finished stringing rods and arranging our gear in the boat.

"What's the plan?" I asked as I walked up to him.

"I saw a few blue-winged olive mayflies coming off the water," he answered. "Why don't we try our luck here before heading downstream?"

Since the float to Cherry Creek takes only three to four hours, depending on how often you stop to fish, we weren't in a hurry. I had fished near the boat launch around the same time the previous year with some success. Because early April is spawning season for rainbows and the feeder creek above the boat launch is their spawning water, spawning rainbows often hold in the river below the mouth of the creek awaiting an increase in flow from spring rains, so they can safely journey up the creek to spawn. The fish tend to congregate in the deeper water just upstream from the boat launch where submerged rocks break the flow, so fish expend less energy holding in the current; it can be very good fishing.

"Let's take a look," I suggested.

Standing on the bank surveying the river, we noticed an occasional blue-winged olive mayfly struggling to get off the water. No fish were rising in the riffle above the boat launch, so we walked up to where we could see the shallow flat just upstream from where the creek entered the river. The flat was somewhat sheltered from the wind, so the water's surface was smooth. An occasional dimple appeared, creating a ring in the water that slowly drifted downstream and then disappeared.

After seeing the rising fish, I knew what Lex was thinking but asked the question anyway. "You going high or low?" I assumed, given the context, that he would understand that I was referring to dry flies versus nymphs.

"That depends," replied Lex.

Not the answer I expected. "Depends on what?" I asked.

"Whether you're talking about how I wear my jeans or what kind of fly I'm going to tie on," he answered.

"What?" I spluttered.

"At some point in a man's life, he has to decide whether he's going high or going low; it's as simple as that. Sooner or later, he has to choose how he's going to wear his britches, high up near his belly button or low so his belly can hang over."

I chuckled and then realized that the decision Lex was talking about isn't a trivial matter but serious management of adipose physiology. If you're a middle-aged man with even a small beer belly, you have to strike a balance between a comfortable midsection and support for your pants. Either way, you usually need a belt, or the trousers may end up slipping precariously at the most inopportune time.

"The age-induced expanding waistline being the driver behind it all," I interjected philosophically.

"Bingo!"

"I see you've made your decision," I said, glancing at his belt buckle.

"I decided to take the low road," Lex explained proudly. "It was either that or quit drinking beer, and that was out of the question. I like to think of this as a construction project built with beer." He patted his belly.

"Did you get a building permit for that?" I asked.

"Thought about it, but I don't like those inspectors nosing around."

"So what are you going to do now? About the fish, I mean?"

"I'm going sneak up on those trout and feed one of them a dry fly," he proclaimed.

"So, unlike your pants, you're going high?" I said as we headed back to the boat to get our rods.

"Indeed, sir," he stated, matter-of-factly quoting the Doc Holliday line from the movie Tombstone.

With only enough room for one person to fish the little flat, I decided to fish the riffle between the mouth of the creek and the boat launch. *With the bug activity on the surface of the flat, they're probably just as active under the surface in the riffle,* I thought, *and the bigger fish may be keying in on the nymphs.*

"What are you going to do?" asked Lex.

"I'm going low along that drop-off in the riffle just above the boat launch," I replied.

We returned to the boat to rig up our rods. Lex tied on a Blue Wing Olive fly pattern, and I handed him an emerger that had worked really well for me on the spring creeks in Wisconsin. "Tie that about eighteen inches behind," I recommended.

I tied fresh 4X tippet onto my leader while Lex attached the dropper. As he stood up, hooked the dropper in the hook keeper above the rod handle, and reeled up the slack, he said, "Time to feed some trout." He turned and walked away, calling, "Here, fishy, fishy, fishy."

I sat on the side of the rubber raft to finish rigging up. As I looked in my fly box for a number 14 Prince Nymph and an Olive Hare's Ear, I couldn't help thinking more about how and when a man makes the usually irreversible decision to go low that Lex described. I couldn't get the image of a big-middled guy with his pants barely hanging on his hips out of my mind.

The memory of a rather rotund cattle buyer I knew who bragged one day that he still wore the same size jeans that he'd worn in college—he just wore them a little lower—suddenly entered my mind. He'd made the decision in his late thirties when several years of sitting on his ass in auction barns and countless hours of driving all over hell and half of Georgia to look at cattle had already taken its toll on his waistline. Something had to give. Too cheap to buy new jeans, he had only one option; he went low.

That buyer's build was typical for someone in his line of work. Managers at auction barns take care of their buyers because they're the lifeblood of the local cattle market, so they usually make sure that cattle buyers are well fed. Many auction barns have great little cafes and an open account for cattle buyers.

My thoughts drifted back to my boyhood. I used to love to go to the auction with my dad. I spent hours just looking at the cattle from the catwalk above the rough-sawn board pens. The intermittent bawling of calves was like singing. Occasionally, a baritone cow chimed in followed by the tenor of a bull to round out the chorus. You didn't have to listen too closely to make out the first verse: "The pens are alive with the sound of money." It wasn't Julie Andrews by any stretch of the imagination, but it was true, nonetheless.

Hands were busy sorting cattle and placing them in pens near the entrance into the auction ring inside the building. Cowboys were establishing the order by which the cattle would sell, the first lots being cull cows and bulls. Men in the back pens, most on horseback, sorted calves into uniform lots to make it easier for the buyers to acquire the type of cattle they had orders to buy: sex, size, and color being the main criteria.

Local cowboys picked up extra money moving cattle up and down the alleys. As a boy I dreamed of someday riding that dusty alley and looking up to wave to a boy like me leaning on the rail of the catwalk. Cowboys were my heroes.

When the auction started, I would be in a seat trying to follow the auctioneer's chant and determine what the bid was and how much he was asking. The cows sold first, beginning at ten o'clock, followed by the bulls. The calves didn't start selling until the bulls finished, which was about noon or a little after depending on how many there were. By the time the bulls started, I would be getting hungry and so bored with bawling cows going through the ring one at a time that I would slip down to the cafe ahead of the lunch crowd.

The women who worked the cafe were always pleasant and treated me as if I were one of their own brood. Most of them were wives of ranchers that we knew and helped to brand cattle in the spring. They cooked on sale day to make a little extra spending money and always brought their personal recipes to the cafe. It was just like sitting in all of their respective kitchens at the same time. The special always included beef, potatoes with plenty of brown gravy, a green vegetable, and a salad. The cheeseburgers, fried on a griddle under the lid of a pot to keep them juicy and melt the cheese to perfection, came dressed any way you wanted. I liked mine with mustard and mayonnaise, tomato, dill pickle slices, and a finely shredded lettuce that I never saw anywhere but the sale barn cafe.

If you had any room left, you could top it off with a slice from one of many kinds of home-baked pies and a cup of the best coffee in the country. Mrs. Mort's peanut butter pie was my favorite. If you walked out of that cafe hungry, it was your own damn fault. It was obvious from their bulging middles that the cattle buyers seldom did.

Most cattle buyers I know were committed to going low by the time they were forty years old. That age probably applies to many other sedentary professions as well. Fortunately for the rest of us, most cattle buyers have the presence of mind to start buying the long-tailed shirts that remain tucked in even when their jeans are barely hanging on their hips. I wish that plumbers and electricians had the same presence of mind, sparing us a gaze into the abysmal Grand Canyon of butt cleavage. Of course, there's only so low you can go. Once your waistline gets so big that it wipes out any chance for your hips to hold up your trousers, gravity takes control and you're past the point of no return. At this juncture, your belt becomes useless and the need for suspenders alarmingly clear.

Farmers have always had a solution in the form of paunch-accommodating, physically liberating bib overalls. The older the farmer, the more likely he is to own a pair. Retired men have a different solution as evidenced by their propensity to wear pants, shorts, or lightweight one-piece coveralls with elastic waistbands that can ride at any level with the utmost comfort.

Lex's squeal, as he lifted his rod on a nice trout, snapped me out of my thoughts on expanding waistlines and back into the moment. I was in the middle of attaching a strike indicator. I couldn't remember how the flies got tied on.

Going low and fishing nymphs is best done with a small float or strike indicator. Achieving the dead drift (that is, a drag-free drift) without one is always challenging and sometimes impossible. The key is to treat the indicator as if it were a dry fly in terms of controlling drag. Even though you're going low, you're still thinking high and managing what you can see.

The strike indicator may be one of the most valuable technologies incorporated into the sport of fly-fishing simply because it makes the taking of your nymph by the fish more detectable, resulting in more hooked fish. For that reason, guides like to use them, especially with clients new to the sport.

John Randolph comments in his forward to Larry Tullis's book *Nymphing Strategies,* "Quite simply, they [strike indicators] allow novices to nymph successfully." Even though that statement might sound a bit presumptuous, it's nonetheless true. But strike indicators aren't just for beginners. Given their widespread use, I suspect that strike indicators allow a great number of expert fly fishers to nymph successfully as well.

Nymphing with indicators may be the most important reason for the increased popularity of fly-fishing in recent years, because, as Randolph says, they lead to higher success rates among less experienced fly fishers, attracting more people to the sport and keeping them in the game. Strike indicators and advancements in nymphing techniques have made year-round fly-fishing not only possible but also quite popular.

I can't help but think that the increased popularity of fly-fishing will benefit the sport. Like it or not, it takes money to improve streams, lobby for regulation, and conduct important research. If strike indicators and nymphing have contributed revenue by bringing more people to the sport, that's a good thing. Yes, we'll need to be a little more tolerant as streams become more crowded, but we can do that. Our challenges include promoting catch-and-release throughout our sport, improving fish habitat, and making more water accessible to accommodate increasing numbers of fly fishers.

I suppose a few traditionalists still consider a strike indicator as nothing more than a bobber and an abomination to fly-fishing purists. Certainly, the snobbish bastards have the right to hold that view, but, hopefully, they'll keep their opinions to themselves. Opinions are like butt cracks; everybody has one, but few people want to be exposed to them. Of course, that statement applies to my opinions as well.

"Hot damn, hoss!" Lex shouted as he hooked another nice rainbow. "These fish are starting to come on." He played the fish into the lower part of the flat with his usual finesse and then netted him. He looked a little bigger than the last one.

Considering the likely depth of the trough that I was about to fish, three to four feet, and the moderate speed of the current, I set my strike indicator at about six feet. One rule of thumb for setting depth: is one and a half times the depth you want to fish and then make slight adjustments based on current speed, shorter for slow current and longer for fast. For short drifts in fast water, I use a split shot or two to get the bugs down early in the drift.

I use a foam mini-ball indicator with a rubber band so I can easily move it up and down the leader and adjust it for water of varying depths. To accommodate that adjusting, I've started tying my own nymphing leaders; the knots every eighteen to twenty four inches keep the indicator from sliding down.

I used to use what Lex called a "Don King-dicator," one of those synthetic yarn indicators with a three-inch piece of yarn folded in the middle around a black rubber O-ring and tied near the fold above the ring to hold it all together. The yarn ends that create surface tension on the water stick up, resembling boxing promoter Don King's hair. They also look like the colored hair on those naked, smiley-face troll dolls. Maybe that's where Don got the idea for his hairstyle. Come to think of it, when Don smiles, he looks a little like one of those goofy-looking trolls.

As I stepped to the edge of the water near the lower portion of the trough, I looked up just in time to see Lex lifting what appeared to be a twelve-inch rainbow out of the water. The trout was wiggling rapidly, which makes the leader in your hand feel electrified and restraining the trout virtually impossible. Holding the leader in his left hand, Lex tucked his rod in his left armpit, knelt down, and wet his right hand in what looked like one movement. (You should always wet your hand before handling a trout so that you won't accidentally remove the mucosa that protects the fish from pathogens.) Holding the line a foot or so above the trout with his left hand, he grabbed the fish with his dripping right hand, let go of the leader, and quickly pinched the hook out of the trout's lip with his left hand then dropped it headfirst into the water. He looked back at me and waved as if to say, I'm tearing them up.

I made a few drifts in the lower section with no takes, so I moved up to reach the head of the trough. My first cast to the head of the riffle, altered by a gust of wind, landed a little short of the trough's edge in only about a foot and a half of water. When the indicator stopped, I thought that it was a hang-up, but when I gave it a quick jerk, a fish shot out toward the middle of the river and leaped out of the water. It turned out to be a nice rainbow of about twelve inches.

After releasing the trout, I looked up to see two men who had been fishing upriver walking along the trail, passing Lex and then crossing the creek. I went back to fishing and caught several more trout, one of them about sixteen inches, and then broke off both nymphs on a snag.

I was rigging back up when I saw the two men, each with a beer in his hand, come walking toward me. I finished tying on the second nymph about the time they sat down on the bank above me. I acknowledged their presence with a nod and a smile and then turned and started drifting again.

"We saw you catch one a minute ago while we were packing up," the younger of the two said. "How many have you caught?"

"Not sure," I replied. "Four or five, I guess."

"All of them right here?" he asked, sounding surprised.

"This is a pretty good spot," I replied

"It doesn't look like much right here by the boat launch," the older, gray haired one said.

"That's what most people think, so they walk right by." I said matter-of-factly. "Y'all from around here?"

"No. We're from Washington," answered the young one

My indicator stopped, so I ripped my rod tip downstream and set the hook. Again, the fish made a run toward the middle of the river, taking all the slack that was lying at my feet. She began to pull more line, so I pressed the spinning reel spool against my palm to slow it down and to apply just a little more pressure to the fish than the drag was set for. She stopped. I took a few steps downstream and pointed my rod in that direction. With the rod parallel to the water, I reeled and applied a little pressure to move her and, hopefully, keep her from swimming back into the head of the run. After a moment, she began to flop on the surface, and I guided the fat, fifteen-inch hen into the shallow water and released her.

"That was a nice fish!" one of the men said.

"They're in really good shape," I replied.

"If you catch another one in there, I'm going to break my rod back out!" the young one proclaimed.

Just then, Lex came walking by. "You ready to go?" he asked.

"Almost," I said. "Let me make a few more casts."

Lex put his rod in the boat and was about to slide it into the water when I lifted the rod on what felt like a very nice fish. "There he is!" I hollered.

The trout launched himself completely out of the water.

"Even a blind hog can find an acorn," shouted Lex.

The color on his gills shone like candy-apple red enamel. The trout accelerated straight away from me and put a lot of pressure on my five-weight rod, which I kept at about a forty-five degree angle to keep the pressure in the butt section. Each time I thought he was giving up, he would take off and spool more line off my reel. His last run was upstream, right back where I had hooked him. Finally, he began to tire, and I guided him downstream. He went past me on about twenty feet of line, and I walked him down to Lex, who was waiting with a net.

Lex netted the trout and then removed the hook as I reeled up my line. The two men came down the embankment for a closer look. The trout appeared to be a little over twenty inches and covered with black spots. He was dark silver with a reddish hue down his side, not unusual for a mature male during spawning season.

"That's a hell of a nice fish," the young one said.

Having a little fun with our friends, Lex released the fish and looked up at me. "Are you ready to quit fooling around and go catch some real fish?" he asked.

"That fish was bigger than anything we've caught in three days," the young guy exclaimed.

I looked at the two, shrugged my shoulders as if to indicate that this was my cross to bear, and said with an air of penitence, "He's got high standards. Kind of a pain in the ass, really!"

"What were you catching them on?" the gray haired man inquired.

I showed them the Prince Nymph and the Olive Hare's Ear that I was using.

"It can't be that simple," he persisted. "What's your secret?"

"You've got to go low, real low," I replied. "Get the bugs on the bottom."

It sounds simple, but going low is more complicated than going high. Even after you've figured out which bugs and what size to use, you have to consider other variables like the depth of the water, the speed of the current, and the location of the fish. Questions abound. Should I use a strike indicator? If so, which kind?

How much distance should I put between my indicator and the fly? How much weight should I use? Then there's the question of where to cast to get the bugs in front of the fish.

The choices are simpler when you're going high; choose the size and color of a dry fly that best imitates those that are hatching or best represents an insect the trout will recognize as food, cast upstream from where you saw the trout surface, and then drift the fly as close to the fish as possible without spooking it. Sounds simple enough, but it's not always easy. Because dry flies nearly always require a drag-free presentation (traveling the same speed as the current just like a natural bug on the surface), going high probably requires a more artful, practiced technique than going low. Keeping the fly from dragging on the water's surface requires precise, artful mending—adjusting the line that floats on the water with a flick of the wrist—a skill that takes the beginner some time to master.

I always look for dry fly opportunities simply because there's something classic and even poetic about a trout's coming to the surface and taking your offering in various and interesting forms. At the same time, I truly love seeing nymphs dead drifted into the invisible depths. It's the allure of what might be over the hill, behind the curtain, or, more intriguingly, under the negligee.

This male propensity to see what else is there is what drives men to surf television channels endlessly. It's part of our psyche, hardwired into our behavior. Lingerie companies understand and exploit this male inclination, incorporating it quite effectively into their marketing and sales tactics. If a woman understands this male behavior and occasionally applies the basic principles, the man is either in big trouble or lucky, quite possibly both.

There are those fly fishers that only go high. My friend Richard Gottsponer fishes only with dry flies. Richard isn't a snobby dry fly purist who looks down his nose at anyone who fly-fishes by any other method. Quite the contrary, he simply prefers to take his trout on the surface, or, as he puts it, "I just like dries!" Even if he were more likely to catch ten fish on nymphs for every fish he caught on a dry fly, he would still fish the dry. He prefers to go high. I can respect that.

Richard's attitude toward going high is not appreciably different from mine toward fly-fishing in general. It's not how many I catch but how I catch them—or don't catch them in some cases. The how is with a fly rod, a fly line, and a single point hook dressed to look like something a fish might like to eat. Beyond that, I don't really care. High or low, dry fly or nymph, makes no difference to me. I enjoy it all.

Coaxing fish to rise when no fish are rising requires a lot of skill and even more patience. That kind of patience still eludes me. Maybe, after a fly fisher has caught literally thousands of fish, exclusively pursuing the trophies on the surface using dry flies may be the only challenge left. If so, I have a way to go.

If I don't see any fish surfacing and receive no reliable advice that the fish are "looking up," I go low. The only exception is in small creeks or shallow water where my nymph won't go any deeper than a couple of feet before it hits the bottom of the stream. That scenario calls for splitting the difference and going "high-low," using a dry fly with a nymph trailed behind it as a dropper.

The dry-and-dropper combination, often referred to as shallow nymphing, is the hybrid of dry-fly-fishing and nymphing. More times than not, under the correct conditions, this hybrid method yields more hook ups than either the dry or nymphing method alone. Like animal breeding, in which hybrids tend to be more vigorous than purebreds, this combination often yields better-than-expected results, especially in shallow, choppy riffles.

Hybrid vigor, or heterosis, as animal breeders and geneticists usually call it, refers to the increase in size, strength, and other attributes of cross-bred species compared with the average of the two parents (midparent heterosis) or the better parent (best-parent heterosis). The concept of hybrid vigor explains why the dry-and-dropper combination results in more strikes and takes than either "parent" method in certain situations. If you made one hundred drifts each for all three methods in riffles or bank water where fish tend to be looking up or otherwise feeding high in the water column, the dry-and-dropper combination would yield a greater number of strikes than either the dry or the nymph method fished exclusively.

For example, if one hundred drifts of a dry fly alone resulted in ten strikes, and one hundred drifts of a nymph alone resulted in fifteen strikes, the dry-and-dropper combination drifted one hundred times would likely yield more than fifteen strikes (the better parent) and quite possibly up to twenty-five strikes (the two parents combined). Maybe someday a fishaholic graduate student in wildlife and fisheries management will write a thesis called "The Effectiveness of Applied Variations of Fly-Fishing Methodology," and quantify this improved effectiveness, once and for all.

Meanwhile, my own experience convinces me that this hypothesis is valid. On a cool day in June that threatened a thunderstorm from when we put in until we took out, my wife and I floated the Colorado River with Bob Streb from Fly Fishing Outfitters in Avon, Colorado. We fished a number 12 Elk Hair Caddis trailed by a Red Ant pattern that Bob had designed and tied. Of course, technically speaking, the ant wasn't a nymph, but we allowed it to sink like a drowned ant just as we'd sink a nymph. Casting to the bank in front of the boat and mending the drift for as long as possible, we lost count of the number of fish we caught, let alone the number of strikes that we missed.

It was a good enough day that when I went to the fly shop the next morning to have coffee, one of the other guides asked if I was the guy who caught all the fish on Bob's ant. Bob was proud of that ant. Not surprisingly, that morning, the shop had sold out of that pattern to the other guides' clients.

In recollection, at least 60 percent of the takes were on the ant, the remainder on the caddis, the point being that fishing either one of those bugs alone would have resulted in significantly fewer fish.

I find the dry-dropper method especially effective when I fish the very small dry flies in broken water. "No-see-ums," I call them, because they're so difficult to see on rough, choppy water surfaces, especially when I'm casting some distance. Tying the smaller fly behind a larger Elk Hair Caddis or Stimulator that I can see allows me to follow the drift of the smaller fly. The larger fly not only serves as a strike indicator, it also occasionally induces a take during a drift, and I catch a fish that I might not have caught otherwise. Not surprisingly, dry-and-dropper combinations are very popular and often employed in shallower water wherever fishing with multiple hooks is allowed. I seldom fish a dry fly anymore without a trailer of some kind unless the fish are very active on the surface.

Before I reach the water, I usually have a good idea whether I'll start the day fishing a particular dry fly or begin with a specific nymph. The time of the year, the stream, and the weather conditions are factors used to predict the most likely successful scenario. A stream's seasonal hatch chart (available in books and, for some streams, online) shows which insects are most likely to be active at a particular time of year, and, consequently, which flies are most likely to be effective. If I throw in the weather variable and the time of day, I can easily narrow my choices to a manageable few.

The only remaining question is whether to fish that bug high in its adult stage, or low as a nymph, larva, or pupa. A fly fisher with at least a passing interest in hooking fish under a variety of circumstances must be adaptable. If you step up to the stream and fish are rising, it's obvious that you need to go high. If not, your best choice may be to go low.

On the same trip to Colorado I was reminded of the value of going high-low and fishing the dry fly and the dropper simultaneously. Bert and I stopped to fish the Dream Stream, a section of the South Platte River between Spinney and Eleven Mile Reservoirs in Park County. This nearly four-mile-long catch-and-release tailwater fishery (a tailwater is a stretch of river below a dam) meanders through a flat, grassy meadow, a characteristic setting for a big spring creek. With relatively consistent water temperatures, this heavily fished stream offers a near-ideal habitat for trout to live and reproduce. Consequently, the large, wily trout lurking in the deep seam water and along the banks attract fly fishers with visions of hooking a trophy.

My inclination is to start with nymphs because, as a general rule, trout in a tailwater, especially big trout, are more likely to be taken by going low than by getting them to come up to a dry fly. In his outstanding book, *Nymphing Strategies,* Larry Tullis informs us "trout feed subsurface 90 percent of the time and on the surface 10 percent of the time." With that ratio, the chances are you'll have greater success going low than going high.

While I was rigging up in the parking lot preparing to fish the Dream Stream, a young man came walking up from the river. We exchanged the usual pleasantries, which always include the state of the fishing.

More often than not, it's easier to ask someone how to fish the water than exercise some elaborate decision-making process, particularly when it's your first time on a particular river or stream. One of the things I like about the fly-fishing culture is that the vast majority of people in it are more than willing to share their experience and help a fellow catch-and-release fly fisher succeed. That said, they probably won't share all of their secrets, and don't expect them to share the location of their secret honey holes; there's only so much benevolence any sport can stand.

He told me that the fish were down and that he'd been most successful with dead-drifted caddis larvae. His advice fit well with my expectation that the tailwater from a lake that produces sufficient algae will be a haven for free-living caddis. Advice that fits your paradigms is nothing short of brilliant.

Bert decided to take her book and read beside the river while I fished. She put a blanket and a bottle of water into a pack, and we started down toward the river. I was ready for some action, and she was ready for some late morning relaxation near a pretty stream. The sun was bright and high. Fortunately and surprisingly, there was little wind, which can be problematic to fly fishers in this high mountain valley.

A few fly fishers were scattered out both up- and downstream. No fish were rising in the big flat in front of me, so I waded into the water and fished the far undercut bank. Stream banks become undercut when the soil under the roots of grass along bank erodes. Fish often lie against an undercut bank where the current is slower waiting to ambush passing bugs. After thirty minutes or so without a bite, I decided to move down below an S-bend where the rocks and gravel created the kind of habitat that trout like. Bert liked her spot, so she stayed put while I traipsed off downstream.

Three other men were fishing around the first curve of the S-bend. I crossed in the shallow riffle between the two bends about thirty yards below some gray, decaying pylons from an old wooden bridge. The water below the riffle was deep and, judging by the turbulent, braided surface, there were some large rocks on the bottom. This hole made a ninety-degree turn against a steep bank as it tailed out to a two-foot-deep riffle.

I slid my orange foam strike indicator up the leader to allow for about ten feet between it and the nymphs and spent an hour or so carefully working all that water without as much as a bump. I decided to work the riffle below the second bend. The riffle was very choppy, and, even with only two feet of water, I couldn't easily see the bottom or any fish in the flow.

This riffle was exactly the kind that Dave Hughes describes in *Reading the Water: A Fly Fisherman's Handbook for Finding Trout in All Types of Water* as ideal for the dry-fly-and-nymph-dropper combination. Not wanting to take time to tie on the dry fly, I just slid the bright orange indicator down to within about four feet of the bottom nymph, hoping that it wouldn't spook the fish. I was also relying on the premise that fish in frequently fished catch-and-release streams become accustomed to seeing—and thus desensitized to the presence of—fly line, strike indicators, and even boats.

I heard somewhere that the frequent use of indicators on heavily fished waters causes the trout to stop feeding as the indicator passes and then begin feeding again a few minutes later. Although the trout don't strike in the presence of an indicator, it doesn't send them down to the bottom, either.

That this description of modified behavior might be accurate first occurred to me the second time I drifted the Big Horn River below Yellowtail Dam near Fort Smith, Montana. Nothing short of an armada of boats went down the river that day. Every kind of drift boat imaginable passed over the fish in what seemed like every ten minutes. Understandably, the trout scurried around in the shallower part of the stream, darting for cover when each boat approached, but in the deeper water, they didn't appear frightened, at least not frightened enough to stop feeding.

Many times on that Bighorn trip, Lex and our guide would float down a run that a boat full of fly fishers had just fished. Beaching the boat below the run, we would walk back upstream, fish the same water over which we had just drifted, and hook fish.

Our findings were by no means conclusive, but we weren't there to conduct a scientific experiment. We just wanted to catch a few fish.

Now, standing about fifteen feet from the water's edge, I started in the near corner of the riffle and worked my way across, stepping closer to the water as I worked across the flow. Several drifts into this methodical approach, I was standing at the water's edge. My relatively short drifts of maybe thirty feet, which were now nearly to the middle of the river, required no false casting. I would just let the line swing in the current until it was almost straight downstream, lift it off the water a bit, and flip it back upstream. It's not the classic fly-cast, but certainly effective and very efficient.

Because the drift was relatively short, I was high-sticking—lifting the line off the water as the indicator approached and then laying the line back on the water as the indicator passed and drifted downstream—most of the way. Just as I was beginning to lift line off the choppy water, what looked like a trout in the twenty inch range came up and hit my strike indicator, making me wish I had followed Dave's recommendation of a dry fly as the strike indicator for shallow water like this. Just as failing to apply the benefits of heterosis in beef cattle production can cost big money, failing to use a large, buoyant dry fly as the strike indicator for my nymph cost me that fine fish.

A fish hitting your strike indicator is one of those "duh" moments. *If you've got a hot one, don't let him cool off,* I thought as I reeled in and backed up. *Time to go high.* Kneeling down, I nervously clipped the knot that secured the top nymph and stuck both nymphs onto the wool patch on my vest. I removed the indicator, slipping it into the chest pocket below the patch, quickly took out a brown Elk Hair Caddis, and tied it on. My hands were shaking in anticipation.

I stepped back to the edge of the water and cast to the middle of the riffle about six feet upstream from where the fish had hit my indicator. After a quick upstream mend, I was stripping slack as the fly approached when a trout-induced swirl in the riffle engulfed my fly. I barely caught a glimpse of the trout's head breaking the surface and gulping my fly before he disappeared behind the watery curtain. Demanding a curtain call, I set the hook, and he immediately reappeared, leaping like an acrobat to the applause of splashing water.

He jumped several times, shaking vigorously. Though his jumping and his reddish gill plates clearly marked the twenty-plus-inch buck as a rainbow, his color was uncharacteristically golden, reminiscent of a brown. Eventually, I guided him to the edge of the riffle and beached him on the sand.

Although it was mid-June, the buck's color resembled that of some males during the spawning season in April. I knelt, laid my rod down on the sand with the reel near the fish, and wet my hands in the clear, shallow water. The red from his gill plates continued as a narrow crimson stripe to his tail, and prominent black spots decorated the brilliant gold side, creating an ornate combination of colors. I picked him up to remove the hook. His girth was much larger than my hand could span; I could see my thumb in front of his dorsal fin and just the tip of my middle finger on his belly behind his pectoral fins. The barbless hook came out easily, and when I placed him in the shallow slack water, he instantly shot off, splashing his way back to the middle of the riffle.

One of the first concepts I learned was to take what each fish gives me. Our ability to recognize these opportunities, to understand what they mean and adjust to the new conditions, is evidence that we're beginning to operate at a higher level on the learning curve. Watching that big trout swim away, I realized that adaptability might be the most valuable attribute for a fly fisher—and a required trait for guides.

Suddenly, I felt empty, as if my stomach were having an affair with my backbone. I looked at my watch: nearly 2:30. No wonder I was starving after such a skimpy breakfast.

When I was a boy, many a day began with a breakfast of sausage, eggs, biscuits, and gravy that could easily carry me until lunchtime. However, back then, our work required greater physical exertion that burned off those additional calories. Since I began to watch my diet a little more closely after turning forty, the big, traditional breakfast of my youth has become the exception, not the rule. The downside is that on days when I'm hiking or can't get to lunch by noon, I get a little hollow. And by midafternoon, I'm starving.

Although I love a big breakfast and could have used one that particular day, continuing to do so might force me to rethink the high-low decision for my pants; I decided to go high years ago, about the same time that I decided to reduce my calorie intake. Combining a healthy diet with increased physical activity, like stomping up and down riverbanks, will likely increase the number of days I'm allowed to stomp up and down riverbanks.

"That looked like a pretty nice fish," said a voice behind me, dissolving my high-calorie daydream.

A little startled, I turned to see that a big man had walked up behind me. The man was well over six feet tall and could easily have been an offensive lineman in a former life.

"Twenty-two, maybe twenty-three inches," I replied.

"That *is* nice," he said. "Were you going high or low?"

Surprised by the question, I cast a quick look at him and began laughing.

"What's so funny?" he inquired.

"I've never heard anyone else ask that question that way," I answered. "I asked a friend of mine up on the Madison last spring if he was going high or low and he asked me if I was referring to how he was going to fish or wear his pants."

"That's pretty funny," he said. "I'm Rod."

I stood up, shook his hand, and introduced myself. His hand was huge and his grip was firm. I'm sure mine felt cold and wet to him after handling that fish. I explained the entire story about how, at some point in a man's life, he has to decide whether to go high or low with respect to his pants.

"That applies to wading belts, too," he said with an air of pride as he hooked his thumb in the side of his low-hung wading belt and moved it up and down several times. "I'm probably packing a little more weight than I need," he continued, "but I try to stay active."

"I'm pretty much committed to going low," Rod said, with his right thumb still under his wading belt.

"Any chance of getting back to going high?" I asked.

"The only chance of that happening is if I get marooned for a year on a tropical island with Jenny Craig and the current Miss Fitness America," he said.

I smiled.

"By the time they rescue me," he continued, "I'll look like old Poker Pete's hound—nothing but nuts and ribs."

The image of a scrawny dog with large testicles suddenly appeared in my mind, and I chuckled. "Then you can wear your pants any way you want," I replied.

"Hell, after that, I won't even care if I own a pair of pants."

"Good point," I said.

My stomach was starting to growl. I stepped up to Rod and

extended my hand. His big hand completely engulfed mine. "I'm heading out, Rod," I said. "Good to meet you."

"Nice to meet you."

"Have a good afternoon," I said, turning away and heading for the parking lot.

"You, too," he said.

"By the way, Rod," I said, looking over my shoulder. "Go high. That fish took an Elk Hair Caddis in the middle of the riffle."

Chapter 5

Gauchos and Barbed Wire

Pablo and I pulled into the parking lot near a private camp-ground on the South Branch of the Whitewater River. Pablo is from Argentina and graduated from Cornell as a ruminant nutritionist, which is why Cargill hired him in 2002 and he moved to Minneapolis. We shared an interest in beef cattle, and, as I soon found out, a passion for fly-fishing. Naturally, we hit it off.

The winter of 2004 had been long and brutal. We were well into April; the snow was finally gone, and runoff that had swollen the rivers had subsided. This Saturday morning was our first opportunity to get on the river with the prospect of clear water.

The sun was shining brightly as we started up the trail. Our packs were loaded with the usual trappings—a rain jacket, bottles of water, and lunch—for an all-day outing.

From our parking place near a private campground, we had to hike at least half a mile before the camping crowd thinned out and the better fly-fishing began. We saw only two other cars in the parking lot and just a handful of campers, which was a good sign in terms of company on the river. Fortunately, campers rarely hike past the barbed wire cross fence that divides the upper and lower sections of the South Branch. Most campers remain in the meadow stretch that serves as pasture for a small herd of beef cows and their calves.

As with most rivers, the fishing gets better the farther you get from the campgrounds, picnic areas, and roads. Better fishing doesn't always mean catching more or larger fish, just encountering fewer people while you *try* to catch more or larger fish.

Like the other branches of the Whitewater River watershed, the South Branch is cut from forested limestone canyons fed by countless springs along its length, which provide an ideal environment for aquatic insects—and for the naturally reproducing brown trout that feed on them.

The upper reaches of the South Branch have the typical riffle, run, hole structure that Hughes describes in *Reading the Water.* Just as Hughes predicts, we found a good bit of flat water where the spin casters and bait anglers lurk when the trout season opens in April. Occasionally, they will catch a trout in deep, fast-moving riffles or runs early in the season when the trout are hungry, but once the caddisflies start hatching, those methods are considerably less effective. Most of those anglers lose interest in trout by the second weekend in May, which, coincidentally, is the first day of walleyed pike season in Minnesota. At that point, they generally move from the rivers to the lakes where the walleye lurk.

We kept our four-piece rods, with the reels attached, in two pieces for the hike, as it's easier to hike with it that way. Late April can bring a variety of hatching insects, including blue-winged olives and caddis in a multitude of colors, so we generally wait to tie on flies until we reach the water we want to fish. Of course, if we had tied on either of those bugs as nymphs or dry flies before getting to the water, then, as sure as it was daylight, the other one would be coming off the water when we reached the stretch of the river that we wanted to fish.

Clear, sunny days with low humidity, like that day, generally don't produce significant mayfly activity, but we knew that if the clouds rolled in, the mayfly nymphs would become active, and, by noon, we could very likely have a stem-winder of a hatch.

Stoneflies are another possible choice for a fly to use this time of year. In early spring, stonefly nymphs migrate by crawling along the river bottom to shore where they morph into the adult stage on land. During this migration from the faster water where they spend most of their lives, stonefly nymphs get swept away from the rocks as they crawl along the bottom. Because they are poor swimmers, stonefly nymphs that become dislodged drift helplessly in the current making them an easy target for hungry trout.

The foliage was beginning to come alive with the emerging colors of a typical Midwest spring. The emerald grass was just long enough to provide a little nourishment for the few Black Baldy cows scattered across the pasture between the campground and the first river crossing.

As we walked the bank to the first crossing, I reached out and shook the streamside willows. Partially developed, almost fluorescent, chartreuse leaves came alive with the fluttering of small, light brown caddisflies, a good sign of what the day might offer.

Wading in the shallow riffle where the trail first crossed the river, I stopped, pulled up my sleeve, knelt down, and picked up a rock to see which aquatic fauna were present and potentially active. The shallow, chatty riffle grew louder as I bent closer, and the cold, gin-clear water made goose bumps stand up on my forearm. Grasping a fist-sized rock, I raised it and flipped down the magnifying glasses attached to the bill of my cap.

After turning the rock over and bringing it into focus, I saw a number of small, wriggling, olive-colored nymphs, but the absence of darkened wing pads dampened my hopes for a mayfly hatch. Pablo picked up a rock and showed me a grayish tan, free-living caddis larva. That sight was encouraging, especially considering the caddis that had fluttered from the willows when we shook them.

"Looks like the caddis are it," I said, "at least for this morning."

Dropping the rocks, we slogged our way to the far bank and onto the trail as a black, motley-faced cow looked on curiously. Her nursing calf, the milk that seeped from the corner of his mouth frothing to the texture of freshly whipped meringue, was oblivious to our presence. He wasn't about to let two idiots wearing oversized boots and baggy pants and carrying funny-looking sticks interrupt his breakfast.

Budding oak trees and cottonwoods began to encroach into the pasture as we ventured farther up the river. As we broke through a small patch of cottonwood trees about half a mile above the campground, we could see a weathered, gray, wooden stile over the barbed wire cross-fence.

The stile was a major convenience for fly fishers. Crossing through a barbed wire fence is the fastest way I know to ruin a pair of breathable waders. The short, ice-pick-like barbs tend to come alive as you reach your wader-covered leg through. This stile has probably saved more than a few pairs of waders.

Most of the spring creeks and rivers that I've fished have been in the West on cattle ranches where barbed wire is commonplace. Barbed wire is the most cost-effective way to fence large tracts of land to control cattle grazing.

Joseph F. Glidden's 1874 invention changed the beef business forever by helping to bring about the end of open-range grazing. Although others had developed wire with points to restrain cattle, Glidden's barbed wire could be mass-produced, making it affordable to fence much larger areas than before. As a result, intensive animal husbandry on a much grander scale became practical.

Like most radically new technologies that challenge traditional paradigms, barbed wire was controversial. Religious groups called it "the work of the devil" because of the injuries it often inflicted on wild cattle on their first encounter with it. Today's more docile cattle, carefully bred and gently handled, rarely injure themselves on barbed wire. I suspect that barbed wire cuts more people than cattle as anyone who has built or repaired barbed wire fences can attest.

Barbed wire is ubiquitous on the ranches of Northern California and Southern Oregon where I grew up. Before turning cattle into pastures or range country, my father and I had to ride fences to check for downed or broken strands. Often, while checking these fences, we would encounter the remnants of feeding loggerhead shrikes *(Lanius ludovicianus)*.

Known for its ability to catch insects, the shrike is an unimposing bird with a slightly hooked beak and black feathers around the eyes that form what looks like a Lone Ranger mask. Like other species of shrikes around the world, the loggerhead impales its food on thorns or barbs. In summer, it often skewers grasshoppers on the barbed wire fences, crucifying them, so to speak. The thorn or barb holds the quarry as the shrike pulls bite-size pieces from the carcass. The uneaten remnants dry out to become what amounts to grasshopper jerky.

Ranchers concerned with conservation can use barbed wire to manage streamside erosion where livestock have unlimited access to sensitive, erosion-prone banks. To protect the banks, many ranchers now fence the streams and allow cattle access to the stream only from specific points. Confining cattle to gently sloping or rocky ground for drinking from and crossing the stream substantially decreases bank erosion, conserving soil and preserving riparian habitats.

More concerned at the moment with fishing than with the

history of barbed wire, I tested the stile by stepping on the first rung and shaking it with my free hand. It creaked with a deep, solid sound and barely moved. Considering the cracked, faded gray wood, the stile was surprisingly stable.

Trees became increasingly denser on the other side of the fence. In the open areas, grass began yielding to a myriad of shrubs, their omnipresent buds swollen by the warming temperatures of early spring. As we hiked, the canyon narrowed considerably. Last year's dingy brown grass lined the riverbanks, flattened by the recently melted winter snow, and provided a dense cover for the tender yellow-green shoots that lay underneath.

Riffles were now more abundant and the runs narrower and faster than where we had first crossed the river nearer the campground. We stopped at a promising run a quarter of a mile above the fence, watching for insects lifting off the water or the telltale rings of surfacing trout.

Caddisflies flew out over the water, but they appeared coming from the streamside brush and not emerging from the stream. They were not dipping down, touching the water, as females do when they're laying eggs. No fish were rising.

As we stood quietly looking at the river, I could sense that Pablo was getting a little impatient to get on the water. "I will start here," he said quietly as he began to put his rod back together. He carefully fit the male and female ferrule ends and then pressed them together.

"What are you going to put on?" I asked.

"An Elk Hair Caddis with a Pheasant Tail dropper," he replied in his Argentine accent. Pablo likes to start with dry flies even when no fish are rising.

I decided to keep hiking and find faster, more structured water.

"Good luck," I said as I turned to head upriver.

The trail, worn to dark, rich soil, had narrowed from that below the fence. Vegetation of varying shades of green appeared to be creeping in from the sides. Dandelions competed with what little grass remained for the exposed soil along the edge of the trail. The slow rhythm of my pace began to lull me into a sort of trance.

My right foot caught on an exposed tree root, and I instantly snapped back to reality, my cadence broken, as I lunged forward. With my upper body hurtling toward the ground, my feet scrambled to catch up. After four or five exaggerated strides, it became clear that I wouldn't pull out of this nosedive. My reptilian brain took over and instinctively initiated a PLF, short for Parachute Landing Fall. PLF is a paratrooper term for lessening the impact and landing safely by rolling on your side, using your feet, calves, thighs, hips, and back. Instinctively, I tucked my chin, managed to get my right calf down, and rolled onto my back just in time to avoid a complete, unobstructed face-plant.

Not seriously injured, I jumped up and looked around to see if anyone had seen my circus act. Not a soul was in sight. Even so, my face was warm with embarrassment. Like the tree that falls in the woods with no one around to hear it, I had fallen with no one to see me. I started to relax, and then my gut tightened. *Shit, I hope that didn't break my rod!* I thought.

Anxiously, I examined my rod and sighed with relief. No damage.

Okay, let's quit screwing around and get a bug on the water, I thought as I brushed myself off.

About a quarter mile up the trail from where I had left Pablo, I came upon a spin fisherman casting into the tail of a choppy run that looked promising.

Large rocks on the sides of the run and in the tail out protected the trout from the current, and the choppy surface provided a cover from predation. The oxygen-rich riffle above funneled a continuous source of food into the run for waiting trout. Everything a trout needs was right there.

Standing about twenty yards away from the spin fisherman, I watched him for a few minutes. He cast across the tail out then slowly retrieved his line. I saw a fish break the surface a little upstream from where he was standing, but he apparently didn't see it. A caddis slowly lifted off the water like a tiny helicopter, and another fish splashily surfaced. The remnant rings on the water grew larger as they drifted into the lower tail out. The spin angler saw that fish splash and cast beyond where he had surfaced. On the retrieve, the lure came very near where the fish had surfaced, but the trout wasn't interested. *All right!* I thought. *This could be the beginning of a good hatch.*

I was hoping this guy wouldn't spook these fish, scattering them like quail, which is easy to do. Wild trout are like wary high school freshmen at their first outdoor kegger. The prospect of food or drink drives them to activity but with heightened awareness of danger. For trout, it's high-quality nourishment and a predator; for the underclassmen, it's an overwhelming desire to drink beer and a deputy sheriff. Either situation can quickly turn dramatic.

The first time I witnessed this kind of drama was in high school when a greener-than-gooseshit freshman gained a more intimate understanding of barbed wire and why cattlemen who supported the open range and despised barbed wire once referred it to as "the devil's rope."

About thirty of us, mostly high school upperclassmen, boys and girls, and a few boys that had graduated a couple of years earlier had parked at the end of a dirt road near the entrance to some U.S. Forest Service land where a rancher I day-worked for grazed cattle in the summer. At the gate entrance, the gully widened into a grass covered flat large enough to park several cars. This spot was a well-known and popular party place and there was always a risk that a deputy sheriff might drive up and have a look on a Friday or Saturday night. The word of a kegger must have gotten around because about ten o'clock two carloads of underclassmen showed up all excited about drinking beer.

Around midnight, the keg was half-gone. The Dire Straits tune "Sultans of Swing" blared from two large wooden speakers wired to an amplifier in the trunk of a '68 Chevelle. A literal boom box on wheels, the car's sound system designed for just such an occasion.

Most of the partiers were already present, so we viewed any lights coming up the road with suspicion but the more experienced kids felt little concern. As some headlights flashed through the trees, a particularly nervous rookie yelled, "It's the cops!"

Suddenly a numb-nuts freshman, scared shitless by the other kid's words, took off through the trees at a dead run. Seconds after he disappeared from sight, we heard the screeching of rusty barbed wire pulling through fence staples. He let out a short, agonizing grunt as his forward progress came to an abrupt halt, followed instantaneously by the thud of his body hitting the ground.

The older and more morbid-minded kids begin to laugh hysterically, drowning out the moans of agony precipitated by the torn flesh of our as-yet unidentified runner. The upperclassmen knew from experience that although barbed wire often caused multiple lacerations requiring stitches, it rarely caused serious injury.

Many other underclassmen frantically scurried around, looking for a place to hide, as the more experienced partiers loaded the keg into the trunk of a car belonging to someone over twenty-one.

The deputy sheriff pulled up, got out of his car, and started checking IDs with a long, black-handled flashlight that could easily have doubled as a billy club, and, I suspected, often had. As usual, the deputy lacked the immediate means and apparent willingness to arrest thirty-plus people, especially so far from civilization, so he simply broke up the party by telling everyone to go home.

Staggering and holding his head, the runner came out of the brush. Rust-colored horizontal stripes adorned his tattered T-shirt. Several of his classmates ran to help him but nervously backed away from him when the deputy walked up, the flashlight shining first on the boy's ragged shirt and then in his face.

"Where've you been, son?" the deputy asked.

"Had to take a crap," the freshman replied.

"Couldn't you find something better to wipe with than barbed wire?" offered the deputy.

I laughed out loud. You have to love a deputy with a sense of humor.

Chuckling at that memory, I quietly sat down on a fallen tree and tied a tan Bead Head Soft Hackle Hare's Ear on 4X tippet, finishing out the rig with a tan caddis larva on 5X tippet as a dropper about eighteen inches below the Hare's Ear. The Soft Hackle Hare's Ear imitated the pupa stage of the caddis life cycle, which the trout were chasing. I attached a bright orange strike indicator about six feet up from the bottom fly.

As I stood up the spin fisherman looked around at me. I nodded and hooked the bottom fly on the hook keeper. He began reeling in as I walked up to him and stopped cranking when the spinner lodged securely against his rod tip.

"Any luck?" I asked.

"Got one strike downriver earlier but nothing here," he lamented. "They're jumping all over the place, but I can't get a hit.

Have you done any good?"

"Haven't wet a line," I said.

"I'm done here," he said. "It's all yours."

I could feel him watching me as I stepped to the edge of the tail out. I flipped my bugs in the shallow water near my wading boots, wetting them, so they would sink faster on the first few drifts. I knelt down and pinched the water into them to make sure that they were soaked, stood up, and then stripped twenty feet of line from the reel.

The fish weren't "jumping all over the place," but occasionally one would intermittently break the surface. I probably could have tied on a dry fly, but I didn't want to switch now.

The first cast landed about eight feet upstream and two or three feet beyond where a rising trout had just broken the surface. Because the main current in the center of the run was faster than the current on the far side where the fish was rising, I made a quick upstream mend of the bright green fly line to move the orange indicator directly upstream from where the trout had surfaced. I lifted some slack off the water and began stripping, following the strike indicator with my rod tip.

The indicator was about two feet past where the fish had risen when it went completely under water. I lifted my rod, and the fish darted for the far side. He was quite a scrapper, but after a couple of minutes, I netted the fat, thirteen-inch brown and released him back to the water.

"You're not going to keep him?" he hollered.

What? I thought. *Didn't you just see me let the fish go?*

The comedian Bill Engvall's "Here's your sign" routine flashed through my mind, but frankly, I'm not nearly quick-witted enough to produce a response matching Bill's standard. Since then, with time to think about it, I've come up with one:

"Oh, he wanted to be fresh for dinner, so we agreed to meet here later for an intimate shore lunch. Here's your sign."

"No," I said, turning back. "I can't remember the last time I kept a trout. It's been years. I would just as soon leave them for others to enjoy, too."

A freshly caught fish fried on the shore shortly after it's caught tastes great, but my first choice on fishing trips is a good steak in town, which supports the local economy and the beef industry. The alternative is to keep the trout, drag him around on a stringer all day, and then try to convince myself that a fish in full rigor mortis after several hours out of the water will even come close to a USDA Choice rib eye augmented with garlic, salt, and pepper and then grilled to medium rare perfection. No contest.

I stood up and sent another cast in the same general direction as the first. During the drift, a fish surfaced in the lower end of the run not fifteen feet from me, so my next cast was into the middle of the run just up from where that one had surfaced. I was beginning to raise my rod to high stick the middle portion of the drift when my indicator stopped. Another nice, fat brown appeared. I guided this fish into the tail out of the run to tire him so he wouldn't spook the fish further upstream, which were beginning to rise with increasing frequency.

I netted the fish, a near carbon copy of the first, his bright white belly gradually yielding to bright gold on the sides. Black spots decorated the gold and then became almost indistinguishable as they blended with the darker dorsal region. I held his plump, firm belly, indicative of a well-fed trout, as I removed the hook. Releasing the fish, I looked back to see if my spin-fishing friend was still there.

"Nice fish," he said as he turned and headed downstream.

Even though I enjoy fishing alone, having that guy see me catch a fish, especially when he hadn't caught any, was great for my ego.

A half-dozen fish were now breaking the surface. At the head of the run, a very nice trout, possibly in the eighteen-inch range, had staked out a position to intercept the first of the caddis pupae that made it down from the riffle above. As with most pecking orders, the big fish eat first.

The temptation to cast to the big fish was great, but I knew that moving into position to reach him was likely to spook other rising fish. Even if changing my position didn't send them all down to the bottom, hooking him and fighting him through the run to land him definitely would.

I had learned the value of patience in this situation on a popular spring creek in Montana the previous summer.

On an overcast day, I walked up on a young fly fisher and his guide who had stopped about fifty feet from the tail of a run where several fish were dimpling the surface. The guide calmly observed the entire run, noting the mayflies undulating in the choppy current like little sailboats. Eventually, their tiny wings gracefully fluttered, slowly lifting them off the water in the lower part of the run and the tail out.

The overcast sky and high humidity lengthened the drying time of their wings, requiring the mayflies to remain on the surface longer than normal and making them easy targets for the trout. The slow and deliberate rising of the trout, gently sipping the mayfly nymphs struggling in the surface film or the duns drifting to dry their wings, indicated that the fish were in no particular hurry.

"Holy crap!" the astonished young man exclaimed. "What are they taking?"

"Blue Wing Olives," the guide said nonchalantly as he opened his fly box. "Size 16." The guide pointed out a particularly large fish rising at the head of the run. "Look, that one will likely go twenty inches." Clearly knowing that his words would further excite the novice, he added, "Maybe bigger," as he tied on the size 16 Blue Wing Olive.

By now, the young man was about to burst. Twitching nervously, he stammered, "L-L-Let's run up to the head of the run and c-catch that big one!"

The guide, without lifting his head and while applying floatant to the dry fly, deadpanned, "Let's just start at the tail out, work our way up, and catch 'em all."

He handed the rod to his client and instructed him to cast at an angle upstream to the middle of the river and drift through the tail out. The guide was netting the first fish when I headed up river. They may not have caught them all but I'm sure they got their share and very likely a shot at the big one.

Experience is an asset and patience a virtue, I thought, remembering the guide's advice to that excited young man.

I continued to work the middle of the run with the larva and Soft Hackle Hare's Ear with a good deal of success. The hatch became increasingly stronger, and after about twenty minutes, the small tan-colored caddisflies were coming off the water in droves.

The hatch created a brown fog that appeared to hang over the water and caddisflies were landing all over me. They were beginning to get annoying, flying up my nose and into my ears; one even got in behind my glasses. It got to the point where I just stood in amazement at all the rising fish. I'm sure every fish in the run had stepped up to the feed trough.

More fish were swirling with increased fury, their heads intermittently breaking the surface as they excitedly pursued their quarry. Ideally, I should have switched to a dry-and-dropper combination, but as long as they were taking the soft hackle, I would continue to feed it to them.

As I released one of countless fish in the tail of the run, I spotted Pablo about fifty yards downstream fishing a small run in a bend. Waving my arm to get his attention, I motioned him to come up. I thought that if he still had on the dry fly, he could have even more fun than I was having with the nymph.

I turned and slowly worked my way to the middle part of the run, catching and releasing several more fish. Caught up in the excitement of the caddis hatch, they didn't seem particularly spooky.

I was now standing where I could take a shot at what I thought was the biggest fish, which was working the corner of the run right in the seam between the fast and slow water.

I looked back at Pablo, who had walked up behind me. He was smiling and shaking his head in disbelief at the fish surfacing.

"You still have the Elk Hair Caddis on?" I asked.

Pablo nodded as I continued, "I'm still on nymphs. Slip in behind me at the tail. I want to take a shot at a nice fish in the corner, and then it's all yours."

The seam where the fish was working was on my side, nearly straight upstream. The cast was much farther than I would have liked, but moving any closer would certainly spook the other fish that Pablo was preparing to cast to when I stepped out of the water. Considering the intensity of the feeding and the fact that these fish had had my fly line drifted over them countless times, seemingly without effect, I decided that nothing short of wading in among them would stop them. For them, it was twenty-five-cent-cheeseburger night at the local drive-in, and no one was leaving until he or she got one.

My cast began sailing past the head of the run, so I brought the rod tip back a bit, causing the line to stop. The weighted nymphs dropped into the fast water upstream, but the indicator landed in the corner of the run. The slack line fell, curving like a skinny green serpent down the seam between the fast and slow water. I flipped a quick mend to remove any slack from the faster current and began stripping back as the indicator slowly drifted toward me.

I tensed in anticipation. The indicator was right over the spot where the fish had been working. As it passed, I knew that my bugs weren't far behind. The indicator stopped.

"There he is!" I shouted to Pablo as I lifted the rod.

The trout flew out of the water, which was a bit unusual for a brown trout, and then pulled ferociously to get back to the head of the run. He fought in the head of the run for a short while and then succumbed to the resistance of the rod and darted down the run to the tail out. I had to begin stripping line again to get the slack out as he went past.

"Bryan, that is a nice one," Pablo said in his Argentine accent when he saw the fish in the tail out.

After a couple of minutes, Pablo stepped out into the lower tail out and netted the chunky, sixteen-inch brown. I had thought he was a little bigger judging by the fight he put up.

Looking up after Pablo released the fish for me, I noticed that the hatch had dwindled somewhat from its peak, but fish were still surfacing along the run.

"Pablo, give 'em a go," I said.

He immediately picked up his rod and began casting. Over the next ten minutes, the hatch ended, but not before Pablo had caught three nice browns on the dry fly. I looked at my watch, which read 11:08. Not a bad start to the day.

We started up the trail to look for some deep pools and runs to fish in the middle of the sun-drenched day. The canyon was about seventy-five yards across, and the river meandered, hugging one side, turning, and then hugging the opposite side for a short distance before turning again. The cliffs created sharp turns in the river and deep bend pools, many with an eddy or slow water near the head.

We came upon a sharp S-curve with an eddy near the head and on the outside of the second bend. As we approached, not expecting to see fish in the tail out, we saw fish scurry out and into the deep part of the bend pool. We stopped and looked at each other. I winced at Pablo as if to say, *Damn it! What was I thinking?*

This spot looked like a good place to eat lunch, so I leaned my rod against a willow bush and took off my pack. I asked Pablo if he wanted a sandwich.

"No thank you," he replied. "I think I will keep fishing." With a quick turn, off he went, upstream.

I sat on the bank gazing into the clear water. The sun was hot on the back of my neck, and I was thankful that I had remembered to put on sunscreen that morning. I had finished the sandwich and an apple and was drinking some water when fish began easing into the eddy.

I expected Pablo to come back and get his sandwich, but he isn't easily sidetracked when he's on a mission to catch trout. I figured he was just upriver, maybe fifty yards. I thought he might be getting hungry, so I packed up and headed upstream. The river was to my left and about twenty yards away.

The river made a sharp turn ahead. I was sure that Pablo would be fishing there in the pool created by that next big bend. As I waded into the wide, ankle-deep riffle that fed the big bend pool, I looked downstream and saw a rod extended out over the water from behind some partially leaved willows, but I couldn't see the person on the other end. Thinking it must be Pablo, I started down the river to see how he was doing, splashing in the shallow water along the bank. As I got closer, I realized that the fly fisher was a stranger.

He'd found a great hole, and he was fishing the head where the riffle narrowed and plunged into it. He wasn't drifting the entire pool. Instead, he was placing his fly into the fast water that fed the pool from above, letting the fly plunge into the head of the hole and picking it up again after it drifted about eight or ten feet. I wasn't sure he was getting down to the fish. Short drifts in deep water don't give the flies enough time to sink to the bottom where the fish are most likely to be.

I wanted to try the big hole. But honoring stream etiquette meant giving him space, so I decided to fish a little drop-off along the side about thirty yards upstream while I waited for this guy to finish. I shortened my leader below the indicator to about six feet and made a few drifts with not so much as a bump.

The last drift got hung up, and I broke off. As I was about to retie, I saw the guy hook his fly to the hook keeper and turn to leave. I walked down to secure the spot and retie in case someone from downstream came wading up as he had done.

This hole was at most forty feet from the head to the tail out and probably eight to ten feet deep. Trees shaded a roiling eddy on the far side. The deeper water took on a greenish hue; I couldn't see the bottom.

The hundred yards of cool, well-oxygenated riffle water that fed the pool glittered in the afternoon sun. The pool's choppy surface, along with its depth, protected the fish from aerial predators. The rocks along the bottom were likely large enough to break the flow—without a doubt, a prime lie for trout, meeting all the requirements outlined in Hughes's book. In short, this pool looked like a honey hole to me.

Since the water was deep and these fish would most likely be feeding on the bottom in the middle of the day, I lengthened the leader to twelve feet. I decided to fall back on the searching patterns that I've found most effective, a Prince Nymph and a tan Hare's Ear as the dropper, both in size 12. I attached two small split shots above the flies to get the bugs down into the feeding zone quickly.

I began fishing from the inside of the bend, but all the trees and brush behind me made it difficult to get the long leader and weighted nymphs out into the current. The tail of the pool abruptly shallowed to a two-foot-deep shelf of smooth, rounded, fist-sized rocks. The bank, creating the ninety-degree bend in the river, was about eight feet behind the shelf and had little vegetation to obstruct the backcast.

I took up a position on the shelf where I could cast upstream and the line would drift straight back to me. The idea was to cast so that my bugs landed in the fast water entering the plunge pool so that the force of the water and the split shot would get the flies to the bottom early in the drift. The fly line would be directly over the fish, but given the depth of the hole and the fish feeding on the bottom, I didn't think it would spook them.

On the second drift, the indicator hesitated about halfway through the run. The trout didn't want to come off the bottom, but after a brief tussle and some coaxing from my nine-foot fly rod, I hand-landed a twelve-inch brown. Over the next couple of hours, this pool turned out to be a sure enough honey hole. I hooked and released at least a dozen fish from ten to thirteen inches long, all fat and scrappy. Most took the Hare's Ear, but the Prince enticed three or four of them.

I had forgotten about Pablo, but suddenly remembered he was somewhere up river. Now that it was past three o'clock, I expected him to come down the stream—and soon. Although I was beginning to think that I would need to go look for him, I was hoping that he would show up to see this hole for himself. Besides, I didn't want to leave.

Looking upstream between drifts, I eventually saw him crossing the riffle about sixty yards up. He was hobbling along with a stick under his arm, using it as a crutch. He gave me a wave that I took to mean he was okay and would be there in a minute. I decided to make a few more casts while I waited for him to get down to the hole.

Soon, I saw Pablo coming down the small, brush-choked trail that led right up to the pool. I continued to fish. Suddenly, the indicator went completely under the water, the most solid take yet. I could tell from the heavy headshaking and subsequent pull that this was the biggest fish I had hooked so far. I immediately put him on the reel and applied some pressure. He didn't like that and made the drag sing as he moved to the deep water at the head of the pool. He was still in deep water when Pablo limped up to the bank and sat down on a fallen tree to rest his leg.

"What happened?" I asked.

"It is an old soccer injury that gives me a problem every so often," he said. "I just stepped down off a rock and my knee went 'pop.'"

"You want to leave?"

"No. How has the fishing been?"

"Really good! This may be the biggest fish so far."

The fish was nowhere near ready to land. I hadn't seen my indicator since he pulled it under. As Pablo looked on, I worked this fish back and forth in the pool. Finally, my indicator reappeared for the first time since I'd hooked the fish, and then the fish appeared for a few seconds in the tail out.

"That is a nice fish," Pablo said. "How many have you caught?"

"Maybe eleven or twelve in this hole. I lost count. It's unbelievable!"

"No way!"

"Way!"

It took a few more minutes to tire the fish sufficiently to persuade him into the net.

"This fish is every bit of eighteen inches," I said to Pablo as I took him from the net and held him up for Pablo to see.

"What did you catch him on?" Pablo inquired.

"Number 12 Hare's Ear," I answered.

No more than three casts later, I hooked and landed another trout in the twelve-inch range.

"Unbelievable, Bryan! Unbelievable!" exclaimed Pablo as he searched through his nymph box. "There is no way you can do that again, no way!"

He was tying on a Hare's Ear when I hooked another fish just a few drifts later.

"You cannot do that again," he joked as he got up and hobbled downstream toward a small run about twenty yards below me. Pablo may be even more passionate about fly-fishing than I am. If I were catching fish, then, by God, he would be catching fish, too.

A few moments later, I looked up and Pablo was standing in less than a foot of water, intently drifting the short run. Balancing himself with nearly all his weight on one leg, he looked like a great blue heron poised to snatch minnows. The determination of the Argentine gaucho had materialized in him. For a moment, I thought I saw a gaucho's, daggerlike knife between Pablo's teeth, indicative of some serious business.

In the span of about thirty minutes, standing in the same spot, Pablo hooked and landed five trout from the run. The joy of catching fish wasn't anesthesia enough to sustain him, though, and the stress of standing on one leg began to tire him.

"I am returning to the car Bryan, to put my leg up," he shouted.

"Need any help?" I asked.

"No," he replied as he hobbled out onto the bank. "I have a good stick." He waved it in the air.

An unwritten rule precludes one fly fisher from asking another to leave a hot spot unless it's a life-or-death situation. That kind of whining won't be tolerated. Still, I wanted to be sure that he really was okay and could make it back to the car on his own.

"Are you sure you don't want me to go with you?"

"It will take me a while to get downriver, anyway, so fish," he shouted. "I will be fine."

For a moment, I felt a little guilty, but if the roles were reversed, I wouldn't ask him to leave and wouldn't want him to feel guilty about not going. You just don't spoil another man's fishing. Pablo soon disappeared into the brush, the imaginary knife still clenched between his teeth.

After a short time, I noticed the lengthening shadows on the water. It was getting late. Suddenly my right shoulder felt sore.

I hadn't cast this much since last fall, and I was tired. I reeled up, donned my pack, which I'd left on the shore behind me, and crossed the river along the shelf of the tail out.

I stopped periodically to observe the water. A few caddisflies were coming off with what appeared to be increasing regularity. As I approached the run where we'd had such a great morning, I noticed a few fish rising to caddisflies. Until that moment, I had never imagined walking by rising fish and not giving them a go. Apparently, I had reached the saturation point. *This is without a doubt the best day I've ever had fly-fishing,* I thought. Realizing that I still had a half-hour hike ahead of me, I started down the trail.

I was plodding along, my legs feeling heavier than they had that morning on the way up the trail. Even so, I was content and relaxed. The stile was a welcome sight. *Just a half mile to go,* I thought. In my partially exhausted state, I had no desire to negotiate a barbed wire fence. Without the stile, I might have ended up looking like an underclassman at his first outdoor kegger.

As I approached the parking lot, I could see Pablo sitting with the driver's seat tilted back, his leg propped up between the open door and the windshield support post. He saw me coming across the pasture and waved.

After getting a beer from the open trunk, I asked Pablo how his leg was feeling.

"It is an old injury," he said. "It will be fine. I have some ice in a plastic bag for it."

"You should have that looked at," I recommended. "It's going to start keeping you from fishing."

"Bryan, that will not happen," he replied. "I will go to the doctor on Monday and whatever it takes, I will get it fixed."

"Good." I took a long drink of beer and let out a deep, audible sigh of satisfaction. "What did you think of the fishing?" I asked.

"Bryan, what a day!" he exclaimed. "What a day! Unbelievable! I do not believe that I ever caught so many fish in one day, ever!"

"Me, neither."

When I had taken off my boots and waders and stored my gear in the trunk, we leaned against Pablo's car and finished our beers. "You want me to drive?" I asked.

"No," he said. "I am fine."

"Pablo, you can rest your leg," I insisted. "I'll drive!"

"It is my left leg," he retorted. "I do not need it to drive."

He turned, and, using the car for support, he hobbled around the left side. He sat down in the driver's seat, swung his right leg in slowly, and then lifted his left leg with his hands.

"Pablo, I can drive," I said.

He put the ice bag on his knee, letting his knee rest against the door to hold the bag, and then started the car.

As he was backing up, I looked at him. "Are you sure you don't want me to drive?" I asked again.

He pulled the shifter into drive and stomped on the gas, throwing me back against seat. "No, I can do it," he said, speeding away from the parking lot, the gaucho knife still clenched tightly between his teeth.

Chapter 6

Steelhead Alley

Fom the window of my motel room, I peered out into the still, predawn darkness. The wet asphalt parking lot glistened in the bluish glow of the mercury-vapor security light near the highway entrance. Puddles, evidence of the rain that had fallen overnight, looked like black holes in the motel parking lot.

The forecasters had predicted that the majority of the rain would fall near Cleveland, some seventy-five miles to the west, with only half an inch or so making it into Pennsylvania. Based on that prediction our guide was sure the tributaries in Ohio would be too high and turbid to fish and recommended the night before we plan on fishing near Erie, Pennsylvania. Looking at the wet parking lot, I could only hope the nearby rivers had been spared the brunt of the storm.

Lex and I had arrived at the Green Roof Inn the previous night about 9:30 to breezy, unseasonably warm weather. The thermometer on our rented SUV read forty-two degrees, warmer than normal for a December night, most likely caused by the approaching front. Even at that hour, the cheerful young woman at the check-in desk seemed genuinely happy to see us.

"You guys here to fish?" she asked.

"You've been readin' my mail?" Lex shot back.

It took her a second for that remark to register and then she smiled. "Haven't heard that one before," she said.

"So how's the fishing been?" I asked.

"My husband caught three steelhead this evening drifting egg patterns through the deeper pools," she said.

Sounded simple enough that even a couple of dough asses like us could do it. Maybe the claims of great fishing on websites promoting the area applied to tourists as well as the locals. You know you're in trouble when a local says you should have been there yesterday! *Or earlier this evening, for that matter*, I thought as I signed the credit card receipt.

For this reason, we more often than not hire the services of a local guide when we're fishing new or unfamiliar water. Considering what it costs to travel to these areas, that expense would be pointless if we didn't catch a few fish. Having a guide along, at least for the first day, to help us understand the idiosyncrasies of the local water and its fish is a good value in my book. Occasionally, of course, we like to explore and figure things out on our own, but not on long-distance, short-duration trips to unfamiliar country. Since this was one of those trips, we had little time and were out of our element. Jeff was to meet us at 6:30 that morning. I looked at my watch. It was 5:13.

Although not elaborate by any stretch of the imagination, our room at the Green Roof Inn was comfortable and spacious enough to handle all the extra gear we always bring in case the fish are so big and ferocious that they break our rods and burn up the drags on our reels. Lex told me that the first time he went to Alaska to fish the rivers for salmon, the gear he tore up and had to replace cost more than the trip itself. We rarely need the back-up rods and reels that we carry, but having no backup adds insult to the injury of breaking your favorite rod or reel during a fishing trip. Having a room large enough to handle the extra gear, along with other amenities like firm mattresses and fully equipped kitchenettes, made our stay both comfortable and enjoyable.

The three-day forecast was partly cloudy skies, dry and breezy, with lows in the lower thirties and highs in the upper forties. The weather prognosticators had been right about the previous night's rain and we hoped that they'd go two-for-two.

If you've done much fishing at all, you know that a less-than-accurate forecast can screw up your fishing. The water levels might be a little high and cloudy, but, providing that the meteorologist on channel sixty-six was correct, we wouldn't get soaked to the bone or find our rod guides full of ice.

Fortunately, the rainfall had been relatively light, less than half an inch, but even a small amount of rain can stir up silt, making the water murky and fishing more difficult. Even though some streams may be noticeably less affected than others, it doesn't take much silt to reduce the distance that fish can see and, consequently, the distance they will move to reach food, meaning that we would need to take more time working the feeding lanes and holding water.

Since very low visibility or very cold water makes for less aggressive fish, requiring that your fly be closer to the fish to induce a strike, the two conditions combined can make for a slow day, the kind that make you appreciate fresh air, great scenery, and good friends because your battles with monster fish are generally few.

"Looks like the water will be a little off color this morning," I said to Lex as he slowly rolled out of bed and put his feet on the floor.

"Maybe the fish will have a chance, then," Lex mumbled, sitting on the edge of the bed and rubbing his eyes.

"Maybe," I said. "How about some coffee?"

"Thought you'd never ask!"

The smell of brewing coffee and frying bacon soon filled the room. Eggs followed the bacon and were soon crackling in the frying pan like a perfect bead laid down by a welder. The sound of Lex scraping butter over toast as if he were using the knife on sixty-grit sandpaper indicated that breakfast was ready. I'm not sure which is more enjoyable, the flavor of the bacon and eggs or the memories of growing up on a ranch that come flooding back whenever I smell the aroma of that traditional breakfast.

"Let's eat," Lex said as he held a plate over the stove.

Just as we were finishing the breakfast dishes, we heard a car pull up outside, followed by a light tap on the door barely audible over the morning news on the television.

Jeff introduced himself, his soft-spoken manner contrasting oddly with what looked like a five-day stubble that accented his dark, heavy goatee and made him look as though he operated on limited sleep. We handed him a cup of coffee. Jeff was from Ohio, where we had originally planned to fish, so he wasn't as familiar with the Pennsylvania streams as a local guide would have been. However, most guides and guide services have a vast network from which they can glean information about water conditions, fish locations, and effective fly patterns, so we weren't too worried about his competence.

Jeff had checked his sources the previous day, but he decided to make one final call before we left the motel. Lex and I loaded our gear into Jeff's well-traveled Jeep Cherokee while he talked on the phone.

Based on the information from that call, he narrowed the choice to three rivers, all within twenty miles. Jeff's source had recommended that we stop at Bac Bait and Tackle, in Fairview, Pennsylvania—ten miles away according to Jeff's source—for one last bit of intelligence gathering. That suggestion worked into our plans nicely as we needed to purchase fishing licenses, anyway.

Jeff's Jeep Cherokee looked like a mobile office, the dashboard serving as a filing cabinet of sorts, cluttered with papers, maps, sticky notes, the odd fly box, and a carton of .22 shells. As he pulled out onto the highway, I caught the 2004 Ohio fishing regulations booklet as it slid off the dashboard.

"Where do you file the Ohio regulations?" I asked.

"Next to the can of snuff I bought yesterday," he replied. "Let me know if you find it."

Even though we still needed headlights to drive, we could make out the hilly landscape in the misty dawn. The soil was dark, fertile enough to support various row crops, chiefly corn, as evidenced by the flattened stalks that remain as feed for cattle after grain harvest. Some of the cornfields were clean of any residue; only the six-inch stubble resulting from cutting the corn crop for silage remained. Surprisingly, several not yet harvested cornfields remained even though it was December.

We crossed Elk Creek on the way to Fairview; it was running high and looked like coffee with a little cream in it. Lex called the river "blown out."

Lex and I knew from experience that rivers and creeks tend to run high and silted after a rain and may take a couple of days to clear, but we also knew that when you catch a good trout stream coming down and clearing after running high and muddy, the fishing is usually great. We hoped that, just as a freestone stream comes alive with eager, aggressive trout at the end of spring run-off, the rivers would come alive with steelhead as the water began to clear. Finding just that river was why we were headed to Bac's.

Most shopkeepers know where the best fishing is and which water will probably be most productive under a variety of conditions. Since they're more likely to give detailed and accurate answers to important questions like where the best holes are and which fly patterns are hot if you're patronizing their business, we always make sure to buy a few flies or minor supplies even if we don't really need them. I call it value reciprocation; you get what you pay for.

According to the owner of Bac's our best bet after the rain was Walnut Creek, which he said tends not to become as silted and clears faster than other tributaries in the area, so we decided to drive eight miles east and check it out.

We turned off the country road onto the railroad right-of-way, which paralleled the tracks for a couple hundred yards. We could see our breath in the cool morning air as we strung our rods. We had parked so near the tracks that we could have touched a passing train with a nine-foot fly rod while we leaned on the car if we were so inclined.

Walnut Creek, like many other tributaries in the area, has cut deeply into the shale over time, leaving steep-walled canyons reasonably negotiable by a few select trails from various access points. Shale outcroppings lay exposed through the soil on the hillsides. An abundance of leafless hardwood trees adorned the surrounding hills. A thick blanket of yellow and brown leaves, the remnants of the bright red, orange, and yellow autumn foliage that had painted the landscape when the fish began their annual migration back in October, covered the ground.

The sun was struggling to break through the clouds that remained on the eastern horizon from last night's storm as we started down the well-used trail that followed the railroad embankment. The trail was muddy and steep in places, and the brownish clay was slick and treacherous with felt-soled wading boots. *The spiral-wire treads that slip over my wading boots would come in handy right now,* I thought. But being already halfway down the two-hundred-yard path to the stream, I wasn't going back to get them.

The trail flattened out a bit near the bottom and turned into a loblolly of mud holes and large puddles that spanned the entire trail. We hugged the side of the trail to avoid the big puddles, not so much for the water—after all, we intended to be slogging through water all day—but because of the slick, gooey mud in the bottom, which we couldn't see but knew for certain was there. No sense in busting your ass, and possibly a fly rod, before you even wet a line.

We arrived at the river where it enters the tubes—two parallel, arched tunnels, each one hundred feet long, twenty-four feet high, and twenty feet wide, that carried the water under the railroad tracks near which we had parked. Basically, they were two huge concrete culverts the size of highway tunnels, and from their condition—broken concrete and exposed rebar—they appeared to be no less than fifty years old.

The water resembled tea with a splash of fat-free milk added. A foot of visibility, maybe. Jeff waded out in the water, fumbled around in his vest pocket, and finally pulled out a thermometer, which he dropped in the water. It dangled on a white string near his right boot.

"Let's see what the water temperature is," Jeff said without turning to look back at us.

"Looks like we'll have to hit 'em on the head to get their attention," Lex said.

If anyone can do that, Lex can. He can work a stretch of water as well as any fly fisher that I've seen. A fly rod in his hand seems like a natural extension of his arm as he mends to maintain a dead drift, swings his rig to the surface, and then effortlessly flips it back to the beginning of a drift. It's a pleasure to watch.

Pulling his thermometer out of the water, Jeff turned toward Lex and me, his brow furrowed as he squinted with apparent concern at the thermometer. "Forty degrees," he said, putting the thermometer back in the front pocket of his fishing vest as his expression relaxed a little. "We should be okay. The fish should be willing to move around a little."

"Lex, let's go check their depth perception," I said.

"Indeed, sir!" exclaimed Lex.

Looking through the tubes, we saw three anglers working the water below, so we turned and headed the other way. Over the next two hours, we worked our way upstream, taking our time and drifting each pool or run that looked promising. As big as steelhead can be—some will be over thirty inches long and weigh over twelve pounds—their takes can be very subtle, so we checked by lifting our rods anytime that our strike indicators moved in any way that looked suspicious.

Deep nymphing with strike indicators, our preferred method for steelhead, keeps the flies on the bottom where the fish are most likely feeding. As a result, the strike indicator occasionally slows or stops in the current from the nymphs dragging over or getting caught in the rocks in the streambed. For the first hour, we checked the drift several times, picking up our rods, lifting the indicator off the water just in case we'd caught a fish and not a rock. As we continued to fish, we seemed to develop a sixth sense around our indicators' movements, distinguishing the bottom from a hit; experience is a great teacher.

Occasionally, when you're deep nymphing, you feel a little resistance on a check lift and instinctively continue the motion to set the hook. The initial violent headshaking of a big steelhead is intimidating, and if the fish doesn't shake loose or break your tippet, the fun is just beginning.

One of two things happens next: Either the steelhead will immediately launch himself out of the water, shaking his head so violently that he may flip completely over to rid himself of your fly, or he'll tear off on a run that will spool off all of your fly line and part of the backing line as well. Often, he'll do both in no particular order, after which he may come rushing right back at you, creating more slack in the line than you can take up with the reel. Initial upstream runs turn problematic when the fish decides to come streaking back downstream, using the current to his advantage. As the line slackens faster than you can reel it up, you tend to back up, usually downstream, to help take up the slack. At the first sizeable rock you encounter, the ballet in waders begins.

At times like these, your fishing buddies begin having fun at your expense because all your style and technique are out the window. Even though you probably won't hear them because your brain is in survival mode, your friends are shouting "encouragement" while they silently hope that you fall on your ass.

If it's any consolation, they hope you don't break your rod or seriously hurt yourself, but make no mistake, sports fans; they want to see an ass-over-tea-kettle wreck. This kind of experience makes for a memorable trip, and if you forget, don't worry; your friends will remind you. Dude, you got stuffed!

After three hours or so, Lex and I had worked a good deal of water with little success thanks to the combination of low visibility and cool water. We were both sure that we had missed some of the subtler takes.

The sun broke through clear as the noon hour approached. Lex and I decided to work our way back down to the flat just upstream from where the trail meets the river to have lunch. Jeff hollered that he was going to the Jeep to get lunch, so I headed down to see if the run that Lex had started to work had enough room for both of us to fish while Jeff cooked.

As I approached, I saw a twenty-five-foot-wide gun barrel run that went straight along a rock cliff for about eighty feet to a retaining wall supporting the railroad embankment and then turned forty-five degrees into another straight run for about a hundred feet to the tubes.

The water looked like it had cleared a bit since that morning, just as the man at Bac's said it would. A small eddy at the head of the run on the near side looked like decent holding water. Lex cast into the water above the eddy and made a downstream mend, laying the line in front of the indicator to travel the seam between the run and the eddy. He high sticked as the indicator reached the end of the eddy, began to pass him, and then paused in the current for a fraction of a second.

Having been hung up and broken off several times earlier, the line could have been caught in the shale again, but this time when Lex lifted the rod, the "hang-up" pulled back with the classic head-shake and then hauled ass down the run. Lex's reel screamed like a bad brake job—probably one of the reels that survived his trip to Alaska. The drag was set light to allow the fish to run with little resistance so as not to break the 4X tippet.

Halfway down the run, Lex placed the palm of his left hand on the spinning reel spool to slow the fish. Feeling the added pressure, the fish exploded out of the water, the sun glistening on its chromed sides, thrashing violently as she tried to escape and hitting the water with a slap of her tail like a beaver warning her family of danger.

As the fish bolted on another tear, Lex palmed the reel again, not wanting to get into his backing line if he could help it. Again, the pressure brought out the acrobat in what looked like a six-pound hen; she somersaulted three feet above the water. By now, she was down near the end of the run with about sixty feet of line out. Lex started walking downstream, reeling in line as the fish darted across the current, turned upstream, and came up the far bank. Still reeling, Lex held his rod high over his head to get as much line out of the water as possible to reduce the pressure on the leader and tippet. Back across the run on our side, the fish settled near the bottom with a steady pull.

Lex, thinking the fight was over, said excitedly, "Wow! That was incredible!"

The words were barely out of his mouth when the fish headed down the run again. This time, Lex got her stopped after about thirty feet where she wallowed on the surface a bit and then went down again. Lex reeled and walked slowly toward the bottom of the eddy as the fish moved up the slower seam water near the head of the run.

Fortunately, Jeff had left the net behind when he went to get lunch, so I positioned myself downstream. The hen still had plenty of fight and wasn't ready for the net. She tried to make another run downriver, but it was a weakened attempt. After another minute or so, she rolled on her side at the surface, Lex guided her my way, and I slipped the net under her. Lex's first steelhead was beautiful silver with black spots down the entire length of her back and just a hint of pink running the middle of her side, beginning at her gills and ending at her tail.

Jeff showed up just in time to pull his camera out of his fishing vest. After removing it from a zip-top plastic bag, he took a picture of the fish lying on the net and several pictures of Lex holding up the fish. Lex placed her back in the water; with her oxygen supply restored, she quickly revived and, with a flick of her tail, plunged back into the murky depths.

As Jeff cooked bratwurst on a small grill, we talked about how beautiful the fish was. As Lex replayed the event for us, it dawned on me that we had fished all morning with little luck until the guide left, at which point he immediately hooked up.

"Lex, isn't it interesting that we fish all morning without so much as a hit and as soon as the guide leaves you catch a fish?" I inquired.

"What exactly are you suggesting, Bryan?" Lex asked.

Waiting until after Jeff had placed the brat he was handing me on my already mustarded hot dog bun, I said to Jeff, "Maybe after lunch, you should just wait in the truck for us."

As Lex damn near choked on his brat laughing, I began to think he was going to need the Heimlich maneuver.

Jeff smiled, not completely sure that we were kidding as Lex was coughing up a lung.

"You all right, son?" I asked.

Lex cleared his throat and took a drink of beer. "Hell, he's not the worst guide we ever had," Lex said after catching his wind again. "You remember the one-legged guide with the bad eye that we fished with two summers ago on the North Platte, the one who thought the FBI was opening his mail?"

"That was a scary son of a bitch," I exclaimed loudly.

"Jeff, you should have been there," Lex said. "You wouldn't believe it. His prosthesis was painted to look like a big brown trout."

Turning back to me, Lex asked, "Remember when he tried to get out of the boat in the middle of that gravel bar and busted his ass?"

I looked at Jeff and began to relate the story. "I was thirty feet or so downstream, about to fish a little drop-off. I heard a loud splash and thought Lex had hooked a big one. I looked up and saw the damn guide floundering around on his ass in two feet of water beside the boat, cussing a blue streak. Lex was standing not ten feet from him." Turning to Lex, I added, "Hell, I thought you were going to help him, so I didn't give it much thought."

"I figured the ornery bastard might hit me if I tried to help him," Lex explained.

"Anyway," I continued, "the guide was floundering around. It looked like he was about to get back on his feet, so I turned back to the river. I was just about to make another cast when I saw the first decent fish I'd seen all day. He was a big bastard! Then I noticed that its tail looked like a wading boot. I netted the 'bionic fish,' held it up, and hollered, 'I got a big one!' By then the guide was standing up, balanced on one leg, dripping wet, in about a foot and a half of water. I waded upstream to return his fish leg. He was not a happy camper."

"I told him that if he had a pink shirt, he'd look like a damn flamingo!" Lex interjected.

"For some reason, he didn't seem very appreciative," I finished.

"He probably would have been, but you pissed him off when you insisted on having me take a picture of you holding his prosthesis like a fish and him standing beside you hopping on one leg," Lex said.

"Life is too short to fish with bastards with no sense of humor," I pointed out.

By now, Jeff was laughing hysterically.

"Okay," I joked, "so you're not the worst guide we've ever had, but if we don't start catching some more fish, we're sending you to the truck." Of course, by now he knew we were jerking his chain.

"Maybe it's your technique that's the problem," Jeff deadpanned.

"Ouch!" I exclaimed.

"You know I don't think I have any cash for a tip," Lex said laughing.

"Me neither," I added.

Jeff packed up the lunch fixings and stashed them at the bottom of a tree near the trail while Lex and I fished the run along the retaining wall. Lex was above me fishing the turn and I was drifting behind a boulder near the wall on the far side about fifty feet downstream. Near the end of the drift, about twenty feet below the rock, my indicator paused, but when I lifted my rod, nothing. "That sure looked like a take to me," I said to myself.

I had drifted this little area below the big rock maybe a dozen times and hadn't hung up. However, I was drifting nearer the wall now and thought that maybe I'd hit a rock down there. *But it didn't feel like a rock*, I thought. After dropping my flies in behind the big rock again, I made a harder-than-usual upstream mend to flip the indicator close to the wall and back again to straighten the line and remove the slack. Near the end of the drift, the indicator paused. This time, I was ready. I snapped the rod up and the line tightened. I felt the violent headshakes and shouted, "There he is!" as my flies and indicator came flying over my head. I looked up at Lex in disgust.

"I hate it when that happens," Lex yelled back.

"Yeah, me too."

I retrieved my line and checked the flies. My dropper was gone. My top fly, the white Crystal Meth, was intact and the tippet above it was in good shape. I tied on a chartreuse version of the same looped-yarn fly as the top one, the color Jeff had recommended earlier, and went back to the same drift, hoping that the fish would make the same mistake twice. After several drifts and no action, I waded down to the tubes. Not seeing anyone in the river, I slogged down the right tube, my splashing echoing from the dingy gray walls. Fine pea-sized gravel covered the bottom of the tube. It was dark enough inside that I couldn't see the bottom, so I used my wading staff to feel the bottom in front of me like a blind man uses a white cane on the sidewalk.

I stopped just before the end of the tube. The water flowed over a slightly declining apron of concrete that jutted out about six feet from the end of the tubes and then dropped off the edge of the apron about two and a half feet into a deep hole, creating ideal holding water for migrating steelhead.

The line of water coming over the end of the apron formed a turbulent undertow that resulted in various current speeds, braiding the water in the center of the pool where the colliding current created seams. Those seams dissipated in the tail out, creating a smooth surface, broken only by several large shale outcroppings. The constant din of the short waterfall masked most other sounds except the roar of an occasional train that passed overhead. Two large eddies, one on each side of the river, formed at the head of the pool.

Could this be what John Randolph meant by "steelhead in a bathtub"? I wondered. In *Becoming a Fly Fisher,* Randolph tells the story of Jeff Blood and Jim Teeny, friends who compete at sight fishing—that is, to see a fish and cast to it—for steelhead in small holes and the ethics involved in how they do it. The hole I was fishing was sixty feet across, larger and deeper than the ones Randolph describes. The water was slightly less turbid than it had been that morning. Consequently, unlike Blood and Teeny, I wouldn't have many sight fishing opportunities.

I stepped onto the apron. To my left, on the far side of the

river, a wispy, unshaven, gray-haired man in a sweat-stained base-
ball cap was standing on the short retaining wall that projected
out from the tube. From about four feet above the water he stared
down intently as he puffed on a cigarette and fished with a spin-
casting rod and reel, most likely using spawn as bait. His stick bobber drifted around in the current, slowly circling the large eddy.
Blue smoke curled up from under the bill of his grungy cap. He
was obviously in his element. I imagined him, and still do today, as
the prototypical Pennsylvania steelhead junkie.

He barely acknowledged my presence as I gave slight hand
wave.

I positioned myself on the gently sloping gravel bar on the right
side of the river in what looked like an ideal place to drift the main
channel of the pool. Even though it was still early in the afternoon,
shadows from the railroad embankment already hung over the
pool. I cast into the roiling water where it plunged over the edge
of the apron so my drift would follow the near seam, intending to
work my drifts methodically across the flow to the opposite seam.

While I was working the slow water of the near seam, Lex and
Jeff appeared from the near tube, the same one I had come out.
They nodded and started walking down toward me as I continued
to drift.

"Nice hole," Jeff said. "There's got to be some fish in here."
No sooner had the words left his mouth than my indicator paused
in the current. I snapped the rod downstream. Something pulled
back.

The fish darted to the middle of the pool, threw himself into
the air, and then took to the bottom. He was about a three-pound
male, a teenager by steelhead standards, probably making his first
trip up the river. I tried to move him around to tire him out, but
he dashed into the big eddy, flopped on top of the water for a mo-

ment, and then headed back out to the main channel.

He was getting weaker, so I tried guiding him toward Jeff's net downstream. He made one more attempt to reach the far side, but the reel's drag was beginning to wear on him. After reaching the slower water across the main flow of the pool, he came to the surface and rolled. As I reeled him back across with lessening resistance, he swung downstream in the main current and slowly turned over onto his side near the bank about twenty feet below me. Jeff handily netted him, removed the hook, and released him.

Lex started deep drifting up at the head of the pool, but he got hung up on a big piece of shale near the tail out and had to break off. As he reeled in to retie, I moved up and started working the head of the hole again.

Halfway through the second drift, the indicator appeared to slow, so I ripped hard downstream to set the hook. This time, I got some nasty headshaking as the fish thrashed in the bottom of the hole.

"This feels like a bigger one," I said.

I had too much line on the ground, so I began slapping the rim of the reel spool aggressively with my left hand to get all of that slack line at my feet onto the reel so that the reel's drag could do its job.

Any run the fish made within the pool was manageable, but had it decided to take off downstream, I would have been forced into my best imitation of Edwin Moses running the high hurdles over many large rocks. A man can skin his knob in a situation like that.

Luckily, the fish didn't make the inevitably man-crippling run; nevertheless, it took several minutes to tire the six-pound hen enough for Jeff to net her and take her picture. . The shot of her lying on the net looked like one you would see on the cover of a fly-fishing magazine, a close-up of the fish's head with the chartreuse loop-yarned fly hooked just inside her lip.

During the action, the man across the river had packed his gear and headed out. I decided to wade below the tail out and work from a small gravel bar below the eddy the old boy had been fishing.

The water seems even clearer now, I thought as I stepped in. About halfway across, I saw two male steelhead in the lower end of the tail out, not twenty feet upstream, playfully hounding and biting at each like a couple of puppies. I made several casts to them, but they were preoccupied and didn't appear to look at anything in the drift, so I left them and continued to the gravel bar on the other side.

As I began working the seam between the eddy and the main flow, Lex hooked a fish that took a wild leap in the middle of the pool and tossed the hook. Then he got hung up on the next drift and had to break off.

By now, it was around 4:00 p.m., and in the fading light of a short December day, I set the hook on what turned out to be the biggest steelhead of the trip. After fifteen minutes of battle within the confines of this great hole, Jeff slid the net under a beautiful hen in the twenty-eight-inch range that must have weighed about eight pounds. What a great way to end the day.

I waded back across the river, feeling spent. My right arm felt weak and worn out. With the rod in my left hand, I dropped both hands to my side and asked Lex, "Are you ready for a cold beer?"

"Thought you'd never ask!" Lex said.

Jeff dropped us off at the motel and left for home. During supper at Crowley's Restaurant, just a short walk from the Green Roof

Inn, Lex and I decided to follow the advice of the man at Bac's and try the Elk River the next morning.

When we got to the Elk River, about four miles from the motel, we found that the shopkeeper had been right in his prediction: The water had cleared considerably to an opaque green with four to five feet of visibility. The sky was clear, and the fish fed aggressively that morning as we sight fished from hole to hole. The action slowed a little during midday and then cranked back up that evening. We landed thirteen steelhead between us and completely lost count of the ones that got away. The fish used every foot of the Elk River to their advantage, taking both of us to our backing line several times.

That evening, we stumbled back to our rental car, spent.

"My butt's draggin'," Lex complained. "I'm not sure I'll survive the ordeal if I don't get a beer and something to eat pretty soon."

I handed him a beer from the cooler, and we toasted the day. The bottlenecks lightly clinked; we drank and then simultaneously let out a sigh of relief. We removed our waders and loaded our gear in relative silence. It was only 5:15 p.m., but in the fading light of evening it seemed much later.

Rather than driving back immediately, we sat on the bumper of the SUV, enjoying the quiet as twilight faded rapidly to darkness. What a day!

It's times like that when I most appreciate the trappings that accompany fly-fishing. The memory of that moment as we silently relived the day's experiences will outlast the recollection of any specific fish that we caught on the river. With a few exceptions, memories of fish intermingle and fade into the archives of our subconscious minds, resurrected only by their photographs, while the meaningful memories, the ones that involve our friends, remain clear and vivid forever, like those of Steelhead Alley.

Chapter 7

Nymphs

M y friends and I were several days into our summer fishing trip. We were staying in what my cousin Chuck would describe as a "man shed," a small, no-frills cabin that sleeps five and contains the necessary amenities, stove, refrigerator and shower, for a comfortable week-long fishing trip. Between the scotch, the card playing, and the bullshit stories, this cabin was fly-fishing paradise.

During a game of four-handed cribbage the previous night, John, a newcomer to the group, had asked whether any women ever came on these trips. Every head turned to stare at him. Nobody was quite sure how to respond. Most just shook their heads.

"What?" John exclaimed defensively.

Because I had invited John, the others all turned to me expectantly.

"You ain't from 'round here, are ya'?" I asked rhetorically. "No self-respecting woman would set foot in this boar's den. The testosterone in this cabin is like secondhand smoke. A woman might start growing hair in places she's not supposed to."

With a look of disgust and a shiver, he quipped, "That's a visual I didn't need."

"Well, then, don't make me 'splain it to you again." I said. "It's your crib. Deal."

I love women and enjoy fishing with them immensely, but our spring fishing trip is a much more primal event, one where males bond in the ancient, unwritten ritual of hunter-gatherer societies, reliving our fishing prowess in the golden, flickering light of a late evening fire over aged single-malt whiskey or finely brewed ale.

It's not that we don't want the fairer sex with us but that they're happy to have us vent this uniquely male behavior from our systems and don't relish experiencing it firsthand. They're delicate nymphs that, of course, have their secrets and personality flaws, but are decidedly more gentle in their ways than men.

That morning, I had decided to get an early start and hike to the upper stretch of the river where I was sure no one had fished in recent days, at least no one in our group. About a mile and a half from the cabin, I was getting close to the water I wanted to fish, so I stopped to get a read on the bugs.

The water felt cold, even through the light liner under my breathable waders. I bent down and grabbed a frigid rock. My hand was as chilled as if I'd reached into the scotch on the rocks that I had languidly sipped the night before to grab an ice cube.

The rock from the foot-and-a-half-deep riffle was too big to grasp firmly in one hand, and it nearly slipped back into the stream. Securing my fly rod in the pit of my left arm to free both hands, I turned the rock over. Cradling the slippery stone against my hip with my left hand and forearm, I flipped down the two-power magnifying lenses clipped to the bill of my well-traveled, sweat-stained cap with my right hand.

With both hands, I hoisted up the rock to bring the surface into focus. The dark green, mossy vegetation gradually came alive with movement. Several small, olive-brown nymphs began crawling lethargically as the cold water dripped from the underside. Most were about three-eighths of an inch long; some had darkened wing pads on the thorax, indicating their imminent emergence into the adult stage, hopefully later that morning.

As the water retreated and the early morning sun dodging cotton-ball clouds warmed their shadowy surroundings, the nymphs' languid movements escalated to rapid twitching. They began to move with increasing haste through the algae and other organic material that clung to the underside of their now upside-down world.

The movements of other aquatic creatures living on the rock began competing for my attention. Midge larvae began wiggling like worms. A bright green, free-living caddis larva began to crawl from under some dark green moss. I moved to the margin of the riffle and held the rock just under the smooth surface of the water so that the insects would remain active.

Judging from their broad heads and heavy legs, the darker, nymphs were of the clinger type—probably pale evening dun, *Heptageniidae heptagenia*. Although more robust than the swimmer-type nymphs, the clingers have a uniquely captivating beauty. Delicate and graceful, yet powerful and strong, clinger nymphs resemble female gymnasts—nymphs of a different sort, I suppose.

Maybe the exquisiteness of these aquatic insect nymphs is what compelled early aquatic entomologists to use the mythological term nymph to designate this stage of the mayfly life cycle. As I gazed at the nymphs on the rock, mythological nymphs came to mind.

Suddenly, as I was pondering Greek mythology, a second- or third-year golden stonefly nymph appeared from around the edge of the rock. Its appearance startled me so much that I almost dropped the rock. Several times larger than the mayfly nymphs, it appeared to be doing pushups. Obviously, it was on a mission.

The golden stonefly will assert itself as aggressively as the mythical sea nymph Thetis, who rejected Zeus, an action not recommended for the meek. After learning of a prophecy that Thetis would bear a son mightier than the child's father, Zeus ended his pursuit of the independent nymph and decreed that she could only marry a mortal. She married Peleus, a mortal king, and gave birth to Achilles, fulfilling the prophecy.

Like Achilles, golden stonefly nymphs are nearly invincible, but they, too, have their Achilles heel. Golden stoneflies spend three years in the nymph stage undergoing numerous instars—the stages between molts—before crawling along the river bottom to reach the shore and become adults on land. Because they can't swim, golden stonefly nymphs are most vulnerable during this migration. If they're dislodged from the rocky bottom, they drift helplessly in the current, their "heel" exposed. Trout will nail them faster than Paris's poisoned arrow killed Achilles.

Golden stonefly nymphs are predacious carnivores that patrol the rocky bottom of fast-running streams hunting other aquatic insects. True to its nature, but still to my surprise, the golden stonefly nymph darted across the surface of the rock and in an instant devoured the caddis larva.

Aquatic insect nymphs in the orders Odonata (dragonflies and damselflies), Ephemeroptera (mayflies), and Plecoptera (stoneflies) are sometimes called naiads after the water nymphs of ancient Greek mythology. Believing that Naiads presided over the rivers, streams, springs, and lakes and that they possessed inspirational, medicinal, or prophetic powers, the Greeks associated these minor goddesses with fertility and growth. Today, fly fishers and trout-habitat conservationists are similarly inspired, regarding rivers and streams as sources of fertility and growth and recognizing that water is life's common denominator. But they also know that rivers, streams, and springs are beautiful in themselves and soothing to the soul. I like to think that the spiritual presence of Naiads helps explain the attraction of fresh water not only for fly fishers and conservationists but for poets and dreamers and newlyweds.

A Naiad's personality reflects the stream that she inhabits. Just for fun, we can apply the DISC assessment. Adapted by Dr. John Geier from a behavioral model developed by William Moulton Marston in 1928, the DISC assessment profiles four behavioral styles—dominance, influence, steadiness, and conscientiousness—each with distinct and predictable patterns of observable behavior.

Nymphs that inhabit fast-flowing, powerful rivers, for example, would have high dominance scores. They tend to assert control over anything entering their domain. Their ambitious, determined drive demands your attention. Their pioneering will is strong and egocentric. If you enter their stream, you'll need your wading staff.

Naiads in the shallow, splashy freestone streams, in contrast, would receive high influence scores. Their emotional, chatty bustle and magnetic optimism communicate openness and warmth, inviting our trust. Their demonstrative nature and enthusiasm persuade you to wade in and test your skills. Their embrace offers security and intimacy. Smitten, you'll return to taste their delights again.

The presiding nymph of a more consistent, even-flowing spring creek exhibits more patience, indicative of a high steadiness score. These nymphs are secure and stable. Their relaxed, unemotional personalities resist sudden changes in mood, keeping the flow and temperature of the water consistent. Though they're possessive of their fish, once you learn their ways, they're very predictable. If you fly-fish in these streams, you should emulate the nymph's steady, calm, and deliberate approach.

The nymphs who inhabit well-organized tailwater rivers with distinct systematic runs and neat, carefully carved seams score high in conscientiousness. To extract the bounty in these streams, you must learn their unwritten rules and regulations. Larger, faster tailwater fisheries may require caution and careful, diplomatic negotiation. Accuracy, stealth, diplomacy, and tact are essential when you fish the clear flows of a tailwater; it's important that you do the job right the first time.

Like the nymphs that inhabit them, streams have moods that vary with season regardless of the type of stream. During spring runoff, a stream can turn aggressive, torrential, and angry. By late summer and fall, the mood frequently becomes more tranquil. The cold of winter brings a mood of silent, sometimes sullen yearning.

I replaced the rock in the stream and waded to the far bank. I stepped up onto the trail, turned and looked out over the rippling water A feeling of tranquil intimacy embraced me like the arms of a woman. I paused soaking in the moment as the sun glistened of the riffle below, then slowly turned and headed upstream.

The river made a large bend ahead, so I cut through an open, sun-drenched clearing with only knee-high vegetation. Leaving the sight of the water took extra effort as if I were resisting the pull of some mild electromagnetic field. Like an insecure teenage boy on a date with a popular girl, I didn't want to get too far away from my nymph and her stream.

The short brush in the clearing scratched against my waders like Acantha scratching Apollo's face as she resisted his advances. I silently hoped that the brush hadn't torn a hole in my waders.

The boughs hanging from the spruce trunks swayed in a gentle morning breeze like the infant Zeus's cradle rocked by his nurse, Adamanthaea. As I entered the trees and looked back to catch a fleeting glimpse of the river, a light breeze caressed my face. Like the voice of the most famous nymph, Echo, it whispered softly, touching my cheek with a gentle kiss. The watery spirit of the Naiad beckoned like a mistress, drawing me back to her.

The creators of these myths, I realized, were trying to explain the world around them in a fanciful way. Even today, fiction is entertaining and harmless unless the author begins confusing fiction and nonfiction, which seems to happen all too often in political or tabloid writing. Fiction writers are experts at MSU—making shit up. I suspect that, like many of these writers, some of the authors of these ancient myths began to believe their own stories, which was probably just as dangerous then as it is now. Nonetheless, the myths are quite entertaining if, like most things in life, you don't take them too seriously.

As I neared the bank, a splashy, songlike "voice" from the run upstream penetrated my thoughts. In the shade of the dense tree cover, the moisture in the air was palpable. The sweet, pungent smell of mint surrounded me, and I peered into the low, shaded areas as if expecting to see the nymph Minthe herself. The plant name *mint* originated with the story that Queen Persephone meta-morphosed Minthe into the plant that bears her name.

The deep shade along the bank was like a veil, making it diffi-cult, at least for the moment, to distinguish any details in the forest around me, not even the fragrant plants themselves. It was a seduc-tion of the senses. I paused for a moment to lift my sunglasses, and my vision cleared. The mint surrounded a seeping spring, and I was experiencing its full aroma. Nature had created a sanctuary, not just for the physical being but for the spiritual being as well.

By now, the sun had begun to hit the water. Realizing that a hatch of some kind was likely that morning, I sat in the shade near the root ball of a spruce tree, toppled during a recent flood. I stared out across the river trying to catch a glimpse of a bug com-ing off the water. Nothing. I attached a knotted nymphing leader to my line to fish the prehatch with a nymph pattern that closely resembled the nymphs with the darkened wing pads that I'd seen scurrying around on the bottom of the rock I'd examined earlier.

A fly fisher can catch as many fish with nymphs right before the hatch as with dry flies in the heat of the emergence. Of course, catching a trout below the surface is not nearly as exciting as seeing it break the surface and take your dry fly.

The increased excitement caused by the visual stimulus could explain why so many fly fishers often seek the dry-fly-fishing experience. It's a lot like the euphoria when that last piece of lingerie hits the floor and you realize that your dream is coming true.

The feeling may be quite similar biochemically. Increased endorphins in the brain create the euphoria of romantic love affairs. Our consuming passion for fly-fishing and the adrenaline produced by the strike increase those same brain-altering endorphins. We become addicted to the euphoria and any activity that creates it. Fly-fishing is as much fun as a man can have with his clothes on.

For me, the fun is increased by fishing with nymphs. The experts say that nymphs and emergers are most effective during the early part of the hatch because the first feeding frenzy, which we can't see, takes place under the water and continues well into the hatch. Maybe that's what I like about fishing subsurface; you're never quite sure what's down there. It's the mystery of it all.

Nymphing is a salacious activity, the erotica of fly-fishing. The finesse of the drift is akin to foreplay, gentle yet intense in passionate anticipation of hooking up, the fascinating uncertainty of what fleshy, slippery delights lie under the current's veiled surface. As you work your indicator like a soft, gentle hand around the smooth mounds and delicate seams prying into the yet unexplored world, each drift is like the peeling back of shrouding, gossamer layers, your indicator gently caressing every mound and fold of water. The thought of holding one of those voluptuous, hidden trophies in your hand makes you tremble. The indicator hesitates in the pulsating current, teasing you with the suggestion of what's to come. A short breath and lift up— nothing.

Suddenly, your indicator plunges into the unseen depths. Raw, unencumbered excitement engulfs you. Your rod quivers and then begins to spasm as you grapple with a new rhythm, two bodies locked in the throes of a passionate struggle, connected by a mere filament of obsession.

The most primal of struggles tests your staying power. The wave begins deep, and, without further warning, a power emerges from the depths, leaping in a dazzling acrobatic display. The fear of losing control briefly engulfs you. Your throbbing rod is torqued to its limit. You are in the world between worlds, the magic carpet ride of angling.

Your rod relaxes as your quarry begins to submit. Both you and the fish are exhausted. You hold the caught fish on its side in the shallow water, both breathing heavily. Tenderly you pull out the still hard hook, then you gently roll her upright and she quietly slips away into the darkness.

No doubt about it, I've been in fishing camp too long, I thought as I woke from this watery fantasy. My thoughts returned to nymphs as I tried to find a rational explanation for the seductive influence of streams like this one and their inhabitants. The river nymphs, I concluded, act as surrogate mistresses that satisfy an episodic and temporary lust. They help to manage so-called midlife crises into nothing more than harmless fun and a few good stories. Those stories and the love of a woman make for a great life.

The surrogate mistress explanation works for men who fly-fish, but what about female fly fishers? Surely, most women wouldn't be lured by a nymph in the same way that men are. Women fly fishers, I decided, are nymphs of a different sort. They have discovered the goddess within. Like the goddesses of myth, they represent the eternal feminine, and yet each has her own unique character and personality.

There is nothing prosaic about nymphs of any definition, including female fly fishers. Women fly fishers offer the same beauty and refreshment to the sport as the water. Their mood becomes joyful around water and they appear at home with the sisterhood of nymphs that permanently inhabit the water.

I've had the pleasure of fishing with several women, mostly my wife or my friends' wives when they've come along on our trips. Occasionally, I've met female fly fishers through a chance encounter.

My most memorable experience of fly-fishing with a woman involved a guide named Brandi. Lex and I phoned a fly shop owner he knew in Fort Smith, Montana, to arrange for a guide to float the Big Horn River. Below Yellowtail Dam, the Big Horn is a classic tailwater fishery that requires a precise matching of the natural insects if you want to catch any fish. Unless you're intimately familiar with the idiosyncrasies of the Big Horn, it's best to fish with a guide, at least the first day.

Brandi was not the typical guide, Lex's friend told us; she was special. Lex pointed out that "special" could mean that she'd ridden the short bus to school as a girl. His friend assured us that wasn't the case. According to him, she was the most requested guide in the region, and she was available that day only because of a cancelation. That recommendation was good enough for us.

Brandi looked to be in her late twenties, with sandy blonde hair covered by a lightweight, form-fitting Columbia fishing cap bearing a Nike logo. About twelve inches of tightly pulled ponytail stuck out through the hole above the cap's Velcro adjustment strap. She was about five feet four inches tall, and although it was hard to tell in her breathable waders and polar fleece, she probably didn't weigh more than 125 pounds.

Walking with a bouncy confidence across the gravel parking lot into the fly shop, her sunglasses perched atop the bill of her cap, she shook our hands authoritatively, said good morning, and asked if we were ready to catch some fish. We shook her hand, introduced ourselves and added that we were always ready to catch fish.

Up close, I could see that her face was a silky bronze. Her sunglasses had protected the skin around her eyes, which looked creamy and luminescent. I noticed a touch of freshly applied mascara. The occasion notwithstanding, a girl needs to look good.

She picked out some flies that had worked well the day before. While I was paying for the flies, I noticed a photograph hanging on the wall of a blonde girl in a cap holding a huge brown trout. I turned around and looked at Brandi. It was the same Columbia cap with the Nike logo. "Nice brown," I said, nodding toward the picture. "How big was he?"

"Twenty-nine inches," she replied. "Caught him on a hopper last summer."

An ephemeral encounter with a fly-fishing goddess? I thought. But all I said was, "Cool!"

After buying the flies, we filled our coffee cups and climbed into her well-kept extended cab pickup. On the short ride over to the boat launch, we engaged in the usual banter related to the state of the fishing. She told us how to rig up to start the day. You could tell she took her job seriously, maybe too seriously for the likes of us. I decided to break the ice.

While we readied Brandi's drift boat for launching, I said, "Brandi, I have to be honest with you we're little uncomfortable fishing with a woman guide." Lex, not sure where I was headed, shot me quick look. "It's not because we think you're less capable than your male counterparts. And it's not that we resent taking instructions from a woman," I continued. She stopped and looked across the boat at me with that slight frown people get when they are trying to figure out what the hell you're talking about.

Lex, now had figured this was a set up for something good, interjected, "Hell, we've both been married for a number of years and have taken literally thousands of instructions from women." *Taken but not necessarily followed,* I thought, but decided not to mention.

"We're not self-conscious about missing a fish in front of a woman," I continued.

"Everybody misses fish," Lex added.

"Then what's the problem?" she asked.

Well, we tend to speak rather freely when we're on the river, especially when we hang up and break off or lose a really nice fish.

"First," she said, "I've been a fishing guide for seven years, so it won't be the first time I've heard that kind of language. And besides, I grew up on a ranch with two brothers." She paused. "You guys ever work cattle?" she asked.

We explained to her that we had worked our share of cattle together and that at times our language on this trip would probably remind her of a day in the cattle pens with her brothers.

"At some point during the trip, I'm going to call Lex a sorry, puss-gutted bastard," I said.

"I resemble that remark," Lex retorted with a smirk. "And without a doubt, at some point during the day, I'll refer to Bryan as a no-good, chicken-necked son of a bitch."

Unfazed, she pushed the boat and glided it easily off the trailer and into the cold, pale green water. In what seemed like a single motion, she turned the boat sideways, reached inside to release the anchor rope lock, and pulled about six feet of slack before locking it again. Then she grabbed the lead anchor out of the back of the boat and dragged the boat upstream, dropping the anchor in the gravel.

She turned and looked us up and down. "You're both as full of shit as the Christmas turkey!" she said. "Now get your sorry asses in the boat and try not to fall in the river. And just for the record," she continued, "I don't like fucking snags and break-offs, either."

Obviously, she saw us as harmless, slightly past middle-aged, wannabe trout bums who didn't take ourselves very seriously. Her attempt to put us at ease worked. She was the consummate professional.

As Brandi climbed in, sat down, and pulled up the anchor, Lex pushed us out and hopped in over the bow.

"All right! Let's rip some lips, boys," Brandi said as she dropped the oars into the water and rowed us into the slow current. As we eased away from the boat launch where the other guides and their clients were waiting their turn, she called back to them, "Remember, boys, you can't high stick with a limp rod."

Lex burst out in a short laugh, pointed at me, and said, "That's why he always brings a little Viagra—to avoid the dreaded limp-rod syndrome."

Everyone on the bank was smiling.

"Hey, what's this crap about a four-hour erection?" I asked. "Their commercial says that if you have an erection that lasts for more than four hours, you should call your doctor. Call your doctor? Hell, if I have an erection that lasts for four hours, break out the cell phone and call the damn police—somebody's going to get hurt!"

Brandi stopped rowing and doubled over in racking laughter. We could hear the men back at the boat launch laughing, too, as we drifted along, the oars resting in the water.

A few seconds later, she sat up straight, laid hard into the oars, and dryly deadpanned, "I don't allow cell phones in the boat, so we'll just have to throw you in the river." She chuckled, shook her head, and kept rowing. "This might be the first time I lose a client to drowning," she added.

Lex had peeled some line from his reel and was shaking it out with a few false casts in front of the bow.

"Now, let's see if you can fish," she challenged.

"Don't let our looks fool you, honey," Lex shot back. "We may not be Brad Pitt, but we can fish!"

"Well, then, hit that seam behind that rocky point jutting out from the bank," she commanded politely.

Lex's cast landed behind the point. He had no sooner finished an upstream mend than his indicator stopped. As he lifted his rod, a sixteen-inch rainbow made a water-slinging leap. Lex quickly played the trout to the boat, landed it in hand, and then released it.

"Not bad for an old guy," she joked as she laid into the oars. "Now let's see if we can hook up a double."

She may very well be a goddess, I thought. This was going to be a great day regardless of the fishing

We laughed until our stomachs ached and caught and released more fish than the law should allow.

Lex's friend had been right; she was special. And her tip reflected that fact.

Women who fly-fish have a special kind of beauty that transcends the superficial attractiveness of clear skin or a slender figure. Like the women I knew and grew up with in ranch country, they combine a pioneering spirit, strong character, and warmth. Whatever needs doing, they're up for it.

My friend Larry Keltner, a rancher and banker in Miles City,

Montana, knows just how to compliment that sort of woman. One night in the Bison—a famous bar and the place to be any evening during the annual bucking horse sale—an attractive young woman in her mid-twenties walked into the bar. Her square shoulders and wasp-like waist commanded attention from a considerable distance even in the subdued light of the Bison. From the looks of her muscular thighs, she had toted her share of square bales.

Her long, straight, dark hair, which extended to the middle of her back, framed a lovely face bronzed by what could only have been natural sunlight. Her neatly cropped bangs and high cheekbones accented her dark, sensuous eyes, giving her a paradoxical aura of confidence and vulnerability. She was hard to miss and easy to look at.

After getting a beer at the bar, she walked within arm's length of us. Our backs pressed against the edge of the bar, we tipped our hats as she went by. She smiled, nodded, and said in a soft yet steady voice, "Gentlemen."

As she joined her friends at the back of the bar near the pool table, Larry slowly turned to me and said, "Now there's a woman that can shovel cake!"

The term *cake* describes a type of cattle feed made from finely ground ingredients formed into large pellets or cubes in a pellet mill. The cake is fed to cows on rangeland or pasture.

When it comes to feeding livestock on the ranch, the whole family gets involved. It's no time for ineffective help; a ranch woman needs to be able to shovel cake, pack water, work cattle, and perform various chores. For that reason, ranching society holds women of strong character in high regard. Having to share in the hard work means that ranch women are generally lower maintenance than the more urban types. They may get their nails done in town on occasion, but they're not afraid to break one.

Strong character defines both men and women in rural America, but women are the thread that binds the fabric of society, not just in cow culture but in urban life as well.

Like the nymphs who define themselves by their relationship to a stream, women tend to define their lives by relationships with people while men define their lives by their accomplishments. That difference may explain why we men hang deer heads and fish photos on the wall and women display wedding photos and pictures of family members.

I'm delighted that my wife hangs these photos because, if the truth be known, relationships are very important to me as I suspect they are to other men; we just don't talk about them much. Savvy women, secure in that knowledge, let us alone about it. And that's just another of the many reasons to love them.

My wife knows that the nymphs inhabiting the river temporarily possess me. Fortunately, she harbors no jealousy toward them. She knows that fly-fishing is a different kind of love, far removed from the love we share. She's genuinely happy that an activity I'm passionate about will sometimes get me out of the house.

I'm fortunate to be married to a lovely nymph who, after more than twenty years, has metamorphosed into a goddess. Every time I see my wife in our wedding pictures, my chest swells with pride. I have a picture of the thirty-inch rainbow I caught in Canada in 2007 next to a picture of my wife on my desk at work. They're both trophies, but only one of them was a keeper.

Chapter 8

Hooked

I f we define addiction as a chronic compulsion to engage in
a specific activity, then fly-fishing is an addiction. Fly fishers
have written volumes extolling the virtues of fly-fishing, along with
meticulous instruction and fanciful tales, but between the lines,
behind the prose, the underlying message is a confession of addiction and the lengths to which we will go to feed it. Apparently, the
fish aren't the only ones that get hooked.

One day it happens—the right bug in the right spot, drifted
perfectly—and we hook the fish we've dreamed about, the kind of
coveted fish that we've seen someone else holding in a photograph,
and wondered if we could ever catch one like it. Everything lines
up, we land the fish, and a friend is there to take our picture.

I was already on the path to addiction when, in 2006, Cedric
Knucky, the owner of Interior Alaska Custom Fly Rods invited me
along on his annual spring trip to Nipigon, Ontario., Although
Cedric grew up in Duluth, Minnesota, he lived in Alaska for several of years, hence the business name. A lifelong steelheader, he
had spent most of his life fishing the north shore of Lake Superior.

After seeing a fly rod he'd built advertised on eBay, I went
to his tiny rod building shop to look at it. I remember thinking
while shaking his hand, *If Santa Claus keeps a close-cropped beard in
the off-season, then he lives in Inver Grove Heights, Minnesota.* Years
of accumulated inventory and rod-building paraphernalia covered

every available space with no discernable organization. The place looked like a Santa's workshop for fly fishers. *These are the parts that real toys are made of,* I thought.

Old, dusty fish mounts covered the walls, along with faded, wrinkled photos of a younger and slimmer Cedric holding trophy fish of various species. Despite all the supporting evidence on the wall, I wasn't completely convinced by his claim that he could hook a dozen or more steelhead a day in Nipigon. I kept staring at the mounts, dusty cobwebs connecting them to each other. When he told me that he hadn't missed a trip in thirty-five years, my initial disbelief waned somewhat. I took a closer look at a yellowing photo of Cedric holding two Chinook salmon. "Caught those in Alaska on the Kenai River," he said. Then he told me that, during the seven years he'd lived in Alaska, he'd flown back every year to fish the spring steelhead run near Nipigon. Leaving Alaska, Mecca for migrating salmon and steelhead, to fish a river 3,400 miles away, is an impressive testimonial to Nipigon's attractions. Excitement quickly replaced skepticism.

I looked longingly at the mount of a hen steelhead that was easily thirty-six inches. I quickly slurped up the drool that hung on the corner of my mouth so it wouldn't drop on my shirt. "Where did you catch this one?" I asked.

"Nipigon," Cedric replied.

"That's a nice fish," I said, slowly shaking my head.

"Would you like to go?" he asked.

"I'd love to go!" I exclaimed.

Make no mistake. Fly-fishing has many benefits transcending the catching of fish: the scenery, the fresh air, the camaraderie, the overwhelming sense that fly-fishing, unlike other types of fishing, is more of a lifestyle than a methodology. However, when faced with corroborated reports of monster trout, even the most reverential fly fisher lusts for a shot at a sure enough "hawg."

My enthusiasm was high, but my expectations were tempered by the knowledge that anything can happen. At any time, the fish may reject you and your paltry offerings and send you home with nothing but a little more respect for the game. The prospect of not hooking any fish makes hooking a few fish meaningful. If success were a given, where would the challenge be? Just how much skill would be required? If we knew the outcome, how much fun would it be? As ESPN's NFL sportscaster, Chris Berman, says, "That's why they play the game!"

I was anxious to try the floating line and deep-nymphing techniques that had worked in other rivers on this trip. Even though the people I was fishing with didn't use that method, they saw no reason why it shouldn't work. Many big trout had been caught that way, and I had even managed to hook a few steelhead in Lake Erie tributaries using deep-nymphing methods, so it seemed reasonable that I could catch these north shore Lake Superior steelhead the same way.

Nearly all the other anglers I encountered were tight liners who used fly rods and reels but outfitted them with monofilament line and a much heavier weight than I used with floating line and a strike indicator. The tight liners cast across the flow and, keeping the line taut, bounced the heavy weight downstream over the rocky bottom, an effective technique but not to my liking.

Unlike tight lining, drifting with a floating line and an indicator allows you to cast upstream into the heads of runs while you remain behind the fish and out of sight, extremely important when the water is low and clear. I was confident that with long, accurate casts and well-timed mends, high sticking as the fly passed and then feeding slack downstream, I could cover as much water and get my fly in front of as many fish as the tight liners, maybe more.

Frankly, I enjoy being different from those around me; it fits my independent nature. I like the feeling of going it alone.

The reality is that we rarely go it alone. We seldom make random decisions as to the places we go, water we fish, methods we employ, or the flies we select. Only the most uneducated fishermen among us go it alone; all the rest have been tutored in some form or fashion. Paul Quinnett states it best in *Pavlov's Trout:*

> *The rule of untutored human learning is to bash rocks together, keep putting out random casts and stray ideas until, when something finally works, looks right, feels right or sounds right, it gets selected, "clicks" into the neural pathways, and is stored in those old neurochemical memory banks so that it can be passed along to younger fishermen. Thus, down through our long history of random new ideas, we humans have selected, saved and improved upon every good idea from fishhooks to symphonies.*

My ideas weren't random casts but rather an amalgamation of experience gained through trial and error or learned from others. Applying this experience to later fishing scenarios improves the probability of hooking fish. Experience eliminates randomness and improves our "luck."

Frankly, luck has little to do with fishing success, or any kind of success, for that matter, unless of course you're just going at it randomly, in which case, you might stumble onto what you want, but then again you might not; the odds are not in your favor. Luck is simply the crossroads of opportunity and preparedness, and experience is fundamental to preparedness. We create our own luck by gaining valuable experience. Those who practice hard at improving their skills and furthering their experience, regardless of the activity, seem to have the best luck. Go figure.

The number of opportunities has little to do with luck, either. Of course, being in the right place at the right time is always good, but it doesn't guarantee that you can seize the opportunity. A fish rising sixty feet away is only an opportunity for someone who can cast sixty feet. Luck, like success in life, however you define it, involves hard work. I had worked hard to become a better fly fisher and the Nipigon trip was my opportunity.

***

The road to the upper Gravel River in Ontario, Canada about thirty miles east of Nipigon was little more than a jeep trail. The first five miles or so of the road cut through a forest, a dense community of spruce and jack pine interspersed with an occasional aspen thicket. Even with the potholes, mud bogs, and errant tree limbs, Mark, a dentist from near the Twin Cities and my fishing partner for the day, negotiated the trail as if it was just another drive to the clinic.

We emerged from the dark, dense forest into an open clear cut created when the main power line was built from the dam on the Nipigon River to the sparsely populated North Lake Superior community. The road turned and meandered under the power line for another half mile before ending at the river. *All right!* I thought as we topped the last hill and I saw no other trucks or SUVs parked near the snowmobile bridge that spanned the river. We would have the fishing to ourselves.

As we got out of the pickup, the morning was clear and beautiful. The air was crisp—cool enough for three light layers but not cold enough for a hood. In the shade, frost clung to the emerging grass like sugar crystals to a doughnut. Only dewy remnants of frost lingered in the open areas exposed to the sun.

Mark had already begun stringing up his rod, his large hands, more suggestive of a dairyman than that of a dentist, made the connections with great dexterity and care, much the same way he might delicately probe a tooth for evidence of decay.

I didn't realize I had gotten used to the warmth of the sun as I strung up my rod in the clearing of the power line until we entered the shade of the spruce trees. A chill hit me, and I wriggled under my layers, trying to shake off the cold.

The air was thick with the sweet, pungent scent of spruce. I took a deep breath and exhaled slowly. The rhythmic cadence of our steps faded into white noise. On the far hillside, I could see the faint evidence of an emerging spring. A hint of chartreuse from emerging leaf buds of aspens lit by the early morning sun contrasted vividly with the dark green spruce. A mist slowly rose from the water like wisps of gray smoke. The soft crackling of water falling over rocks cut through the cool morning air. This was surely Valhalla.

We stopped on the bank above the convex side of a slightly curved riffle. A shallow trough was directly below us. Even though the water was slightly tea-stained, it was clear enough to see any fish that were swimming there. Nothing. The riffle curved away from us, and the flow narrowed into a short run and then widened again in a huge bend pool. The tail out of the pool shallowed to a riffle. The gravel in its margins, no bigger than one of my Grandma Reba's biscuits, was ideal for spawning. Below the gravel riffle, the river narrowed again into a deeper riffle with slightly larger rocks that deflected the current so fish could rest in relative ease before moving up to spawn.

We didn't see any fish in the shallow riffle, so we continued down the trail. In the deeper riffle, about a hundred yards below the spawning water, I spotted a channel along the far bank that I thought could hold fish. Mark had his eye on some deeper water downstream, so after looking at the channel and commenting that it looked like a good place to start, Mark bade me good luck and continued down the trail.

I waded out into the tea-stained river. The channel looked to be about four feet deep along its entirety. It was considerably darker than the knee-deep water I was standing in, and consequently, it was much harder to see fish at this angle. Even standing on the bank hadn't improved the angle of sight enough to allow me to see fish. But, just because I couldn't see any fish didn't mean they weren't there.

My plan was to start in the tail of the channel where I could see the gravel bottom and then work up to the head where the water was deeper.

I had tied on a cheese-colored yarn egg pattern with a red blood dot followed by an epoxy-backed Hare's Ear variant that resembled a stonefly pattern. This smorgasbord approach, which I learned from Lex, increases the likelihood of offering something that the fish will take, especially in unfamiliar water.

Where I stood, the river remained shaded. I felt that chill again, this time on the back of my neck. I shivered, as much from anticipation as from the cool air getting under my turtleneck. I sent the first cast into the near edge of the trough, and the chill dissipated.

I was taking my time, making several drifts across the trough and then taking three or four steps upstream, working across the flow. As I moved up a few steps and into the sun, I could feel the warmth slowly radiating into me, and the back of my neck relaxed. I hand stripped in some line to look at my flies. The trough was a little deeper now, so I moved the indicator up the leader, making the depth of the bottom fly a little over six feet.

My cast landed farther up in the run this time. I flipped an upstream mend and began stripping slack out of the line. As the drift approached, I began to lift my rod tip and then the indicator stopped. I was surprised and reacted a little too slowly, ripping the rod downstream and feeling a strong resistance. *Shit!* I thought. *Hung up.*

Unexpectedly, the "hang up" started jerking back. Instantly, the adrenaline rush began. Epinephrine, the fight-or-flight hormone produced in response to short-term emergencies like a big fish trying to jerk several hundred dollars' worth of fly-fishing gear out of my hand raced through my bloodstream.

Higher levels of oxygen and glucose were now rushing to my brain and muscles. My heart was pounding. The same thing was taking place in the fish's body, only for a different reason. The fish was trying to *avoid* being jerked out of the water by several hundred dollars' worth of fly-fishing gear.

My reaction was fight; his was flight—the classic and primal predator-prey interaction. Even though his initial impulse was to flee, the tether prevented flight, so his response changed and he fought to be free. I felt the thrill that comes from the attempted subduing of a wild creature.

The fly line acted like high-speed fiber optics, transmitting the frantic signals from the fish. I could feel his intensity. Even with no concept of freedom, he still battled to be free. His frenzied, catapulting leaps only added to my excitement, producing more epinephrine.

Meanwhile, another hormone, norepinephrine, was affecting my state of mind. Alert and aroused, I was so keenly aware of the fish's actions that I could anticipate them. I knew what he was going to do before he did it.

The fish continued to struggle, but I could feel him weakening. He was now lying in the bottom of the trough a little downstream from me. I could feel the steady pull of the taut line and even the pulsations of his mouth and gills. I could feel him breathing.

For a moment, he lulled me into a sense of security. While he rested, regaining strength, the hook becoming less secure. *Resting is not allowed,* I thought as I realized what was happening.

I took a step downstream and, with the rod parallel to the water's surface, pulled the fish to make him turn sideways in the current. He dashed out of the trough and thrashed in the shallow water directly downstream from me, making several runs back into the main current, each progressively shorter than the last. Finally, after several minutes, he rolled onto the surface. Keeping his head up and walking toward him, I reeled in line and then gently slipped the long, wooden-handled net underneath him.

With the excitement subsiding, the norepinephrine was affecting my reward system, a brain system that regulates behavior, inducing pleasurable effects. That euphoria is what experts call a *psychological reward.* The warmth that engulfed me had been produced by the sheer joy of winning a fight with a worthy adversary, rather than by the bright sun that reflected intermittently from the rippled surface of the water.

I revived the twenty-four inch male in the slow current of the stream's margin by holding him under his belly and gently moving him forward and backward to pass water through his gills. The fish began to move on his own and then lazily swam back to the inky depths of the trough.

As I crouched in the water, basking in the warmth of my psychological reward, an intense desire to hook another big fish began to take hold of me. I want to feel that excitement again. I need another fix. Not more than ten minutes later, I hooked the first fish's big brother. The fix was on!

It seems likely that fly-fishing addicts become hooked on the chemicals that our bodies produce, making us feel good—a kind of self-rewarding, better living through chemistry of our own creation.

At first, I was reluctant to describe my attraction to fly-fishing as an addiction. After all, the term usually relates to illegal, mind-altering substances or to other unhealthy compulsions like gambling and overeating. But after a bit of research, I discovered that the same coercive chemicals and neurophysiological reactions that drive those dangerous addictions also drive less destructive compulsions. Apparently, any activity or action that causes production of these compounds, particularly, the pleasure-producing hormone dopamine, can become addictive. The dopamine release whose effects we feel when we're fly-fishing is the same physiological response induced by almost all drugs that cause drug addiction. Still, fly-fishing differs from drug addiction as it's unlikely to cause mental or physical harm. Besides, I could quit at any time.

That euphoric feeling when you release a fish is a high of sorts. The excitement that accompanies the drift and the expectation of rising trout or a float stopping in the current is the anticipation of that high. As long as you have a current fishing license, it's all a perfectly legal use of mind-altering chemicals.

The idea that fly-fishing is an addiction may explain those with the habitual need to fly fish, the existence of which John Gierach portrays in his classic book, appropriately titled *Trout Bum*. Addiction is undoubtedly part of the trout bum profile, but probably in and of itself is not enough to make you a full-fledged bum unless you've taken out a second mortgage on the house to finance a fishing trip to Patagonia.

Perhaps a bona fide trout bum is one who feeds his addiction by giving up a perfectly good career to fish for a living. Although not bums in the traditional sense because they're gainfully employed, those who scratch out a living as fly-fishing guides, writers, or teachers of the sport could also be classified as trout bums.

Even if society actually classified this behavior as deviant, it's not likely that a professional fly fisher would enter a twelve-step rehabilitation program. Equally unlikely is finding enough of his recreational fly-fishing friends, secretly admiring anyone with the gonads to chuck it all to fish for a living, willing to hold an intervention. No self-respecting wannabe trout bum wants to admit that he needs a testicular transplant.

The second day of the Nipigon trip we drove up to the power line and then hiked down the clear cut to the Cypress River. The trail under the power line meandered downhill through mostly grass, some scattered brush and only a few trees.

Clouds had moved in during the night, keeping the temperature above freezing but still cool enough to produce heavy dew. The sky was beginning to clear, and it looked as though we were in for one of those bluebird days.

We came to an embankment some fifteen feet above the river, which was running lower than normal because the winter snow accumulation had been marginal and the lake ice had melted early— the kind of conditions that make spotting fish easier even through tannin-stained water.

Mark had stopped to water a small spruce tree that he said looked thirsty, so I stared at the river for a moment, looking up-river and then down, contemplating which way to go. Like Buridan's ass—the donkey that, when placed between two equally proportioned piles of hay starved to death because he couldn't decide which to eat—I was immobilized by indecision: upstream or down?

When decisions come down to only two choices with unknown outcomes that we perceive to be equal we often struggle to decide. There is a rational explanation for this in kind of indecision, irrationality. We have no idea which one is the better choice. If I had known which was better, upstream or downstream, I wouldn't have been standing on the embankment with my thumb up my ass.

Opening the door on one choice requires us, at least for the moment, to close the door on the other, which we're reluctant to do. It's not so much that we want to make the right decision, as we don't want to make the wrong one. And yet, rationally, isn't that the same thing?

Options often distract us from our objective, in this case, to catch fish. Even though we're likely to catch fish in either direction, we can't help thinking that the direction we don't choose might be the better decision in terms of more and/or bigger fish.

My dilemma was quickly resolved when I looked down at the river straight below me. While I was busy contemplating what was behind doors number one and two, I had failed to notice door number three. There, in about two and a half feet of water behind a sizeable rock in the middle of a twenty-foot-wide riffle, was a huge steelhead. The water was choppy, with enough bubbles to obscure the fish occasionally, but if I stared at the same place for a minute or so, I could see his tail movements as he undulated in the broken current.

The water was low and clear despite the typical tea stain found in many of the local rivers. It wouldn't be long until the sun hit that riffle, making the fish feel less secure. He might even move to deeper water.

Not taking my eyes off the spot for fear I wouldn't find it again, I called out, "Mark, there's a huge steelhead down here!" I was contemplating how best to approach the fish with the best chance to catch it when Mark walked up.

I pointed to the spot behind the rock. "See him? I said.

"Go down and see if you can hook him." Mark said. I'll wait here and let you know if he moves."

As soon as the words were out of his mouth, I was on my way

downstream.

I got to the edge of the river about fifty feet downstream from where Mark was standing. These small rivers provide a great opportunity to sight fish for steelhead, a technique that requires stalking; consequently, it feels more like hunting than fishing. The science of fly-fishing—the what, where, when, and how—is now irrelevant; at this point, success is in the art of executing the cast and the subsequent drift, hook set, and playing of the fish.

In a half crouch, hugging the water's edge, I eased upstream. Before getting too close to the fish, I pulled some line from the reel and made a few false casts downstream as much to shake off my nervousness as to get a feel for the distance. I wasn't sure how big he was, but he was probably the biggest fish to which I had ever knowingly cast.

After getting comfortable with the distance, I crouched again and moved to within twenty feet of the steelhead. From this angle, it was hard to see the fish. Still crouched I looked up; Mark, half-hidden behind a spruce tree, gave me the thumbs-up. I turned back and focused on my only real reference point, the rock. I took a deep breath.

The prospect intoxicated me. My mind entered a zone where nothing existed but the fish and me. The intense anticipation of knowing what could happen next had the epinephrine already working. Then the fish's tail broke the surface and disappeared.

Although the context was decidedly different, this state of intense focus resembled what I had experienced in my younger days as a rodeo bullfighter. Before the chute gate opened, there was no predicting the outcome; I only knew that the gate would open, and when it did, something would happen, a myriad of potential scenarios to which I could only react instinctually.

I remember waiting outside the chute. Inside, an eighteen-hundred-pound bull stood quietly with little concern for the rider who was wrapping the bull rope around his hand. Just outside the chute, I swayed back and forth in a half crouch, like a tennis player awaiting a serve, viscera knotted, testicles sucked up tight against the inguinal ring through which they had descended when I was a developing fetus. Like E.T., they just wanted to go home.

The rider slid up on his rope and nodded. The muffled metallic bang of the chute gate latch sent a jolt of electricity through me. The gate man opened the gate only partially, two or three feet. This initial movement stimulates a bull to turn his head quickly. When he sees a potential escape route behind him, he turns away from the hinged side of the chute, opening the gate with his head and coming out of the chute straight rather than jumping forward at an angle and possibly hitting the rider's leg on the hinge side of the gate.

With lightning quickness, this bull turned and slammed his head into the gate, exploding it open. My primitive brain took control of my actions.

The bull burst out in full view as the gate whizzed past me and crashed against the next chute. In my hyper-aroused state, I heard the noise, but I wasn't aware of it. My entire world consisted of the bull and me. Shouts of encouragement from cowboys behind the chute faded to a nearly inaudible din. Objects on the periphery of my vision blended into a murky collage. In the center of my visual focus, I could see more clearly than ever. My reactions were edgy and quick. My entire world seemed to be in slow motion. Fear had yielded to rage.

I remained crouched low to the side of the now open chute to entice the bull to come after me. I focused on his head, knowing that where the head goes, the body will follow. The eye is the gateway to the soul, foretelling intent. I saw no sign of fear, only raw determination. Even before he turned his head, giving away his intent to come after me, I moved. Shifting my concentration to his tail, I ran toward it as the bull's head came around. I made a full circle of the bull and then moved away and up against the end of the open gate.

His head passed me, and he lost sight of me. As I intended, the bull was now spinning with a powerful momentum, which would earn the rider a higher score if he rode him the full eight seconds. The first part of my job was complete, and the rider was sitting tight, spurring the bull with his outside leg.

Though I still focused on the bull and rider, my peripheral vision began to widen, and I could see my partner on the far side. I gradually became aware of the cowboys standing on the catwalk behind the chutes, yelling encouragement. The eight-second buzzer sounded, and, in a nanosecond, I became consciously deaf—and blind to all but the bull and his rider.

The rider reached with his free hand and pulled the tail of his bull rope as I moved in to get the bull's attention and stop his spinning. Like a striking snake, I reached out and slapped the bull on the forehead as he came around and then quickly recoiled. He took the bait and lowered his head, signaling his intent to charge me. Before he could lunge toward me, I turned and headed down the line of chutes. I stepped up onto the last chute gate as the bull passed under me, minus the rider, who had safely jumped off. The bull spotted the open gate out of the arena, and, with his head held high in defiant pride, he trotted out. His job was done.

The aftermath of this primal experience was a high like no other I had experienced. My heart was pounding. Chemicals naturally produced in my body created a feeling of exhilaration. My field of vision and my hearing returned to normal, and I could hear the cheering crowd. The cheers reinforced the euphoria. As I stepped away from the chute gate, the bull rider came up to shake my hand and thank me, after which I tipped my hat to the crowd like a triumphant gladiator raising his sword.

The celebratory illusion of invincibility waned, and the adrenaline-induced numbness subsided. My lungs were burning. The back of my throat felt raw from the rapid seesaw effect of the air racing in and out. Then a sobering reality returned. This bull was the first in a string of eight, and the next rider was already wrapping his hand in his bull rope. *Time to get back in it,* I thought as I crouched again near the next chute, hands on my knees, and tried to catch my breath.

This kind of excitement can turn you into an adrenaline junkie, a somewhat disparaging term that applies to people who are psychologically hooked on the arousal, excitement, amplified blood flow, increased pulse rate, and improved physical performance that accompany having the crap scared out of them. Bullfighting is for the hard-core adrenaline junkie; fly-fishing is for the recreational user.

My line was riding on the current directly downstream from me. I slowly raised the rod from parallel with the surface of the water to about the ten o'clock position, creating a tension that loaded (flexed) the rod. Then I snapped the rod forward and pointed where I wanted the indicator to land, about six feet upstream from the big rock. Target achieved.

As my drift came around the far side of the rock, I lifted my rod, the line pulling the indicator into the slow current behind the rock. You can never be quite sure where the bugs under the indicator are because the currents behind obstructions like rocks become braided and convoluted. Having excessive leader below your strike indicator may cause you to miss the less aggressive takes, and the conflicting currents can create slack between your bugs and the float. You need to be on your game here, looking for any movement of the fish, as well as the indicator.

Fortunately, fish positioned behind rocks frequently strike deliberately and aggressively. They are generally focusing on any food passing by in the current or entering the slower turbulence created by the rock. Even in slow water, the fish know that if they don't grab the meal quickly, it will probably be lost to the rapid current that brought it in the first place. The fish has little time to examine the food; if it drifts naturally and fits the basic image in the fish's memory, he'll take it. It all happens very quickly. The cardinal rule for fly fishers is, don't be scratching your ass when your drift goes around a rock.

My indicator swirled into the eddy behind the rock. Because the conflicting currents could put the bugs anywhere, I knew that I was better off watching for movement from the fish rather than my indicator. Any aggressive movement or flash would indicate a strike.

The indicator began moving slowly downstream. The fish darted forward. I lifted my rod. Resistance. I was just about to give another hook-setting jerk when he rocketed upstream. I was still holding the line tight in my trigger finger as he jerked my rod straight down. I winced at the torqued line. The pressure was more than the hook could bear and it popped out. The line recoiled and then collapsed on the water, with my rod still pointing at the place where the fish had escaped.

Steelhead are the Houdinis of the fishing realm. Regardless of how good we think we've become at angling with a fly, steelhead remind us that we still have much to learn.

Losing a big fish is tough, but even misfortune may have its good side. The Greek Stoic philosopher Epictetus maintained that it helps to develop strong character. But try to convince yourself after a big steelhead breaks you off that this experience builds character. When it happens to me, the conversation going on inside my head is anything but philosophical. Philosophers generally don't use that kind of language.

We tend to get more philosophical about losing fish after we've lost several hundred. We even rationalize the inadvertent loss as an LDR, a fly-fishing acronym for long-distance release. I was going to let him go, anyway, we often say. Nice try. The truth is that the fish just kicked your butt.

Most steelhead are lost because of the sheer aggressiveness with which these magnificent fish struggle to free themselves. The initial violent headshaking may dislodge the hook or break the line. If they're still on, the sheer pull of that first long run may do the trick. By then, all of the fly line has spooled off and you're down to the backing line. With that much line out in fast water, you have little control. A big water-flinging leap that propels the fish skyward may leave you shaking your head in disappointment or throwing down your hat in total disgust. Past this point, the rolling, twisting, and thrashing in the strong current may cause you to lose him. If you get through all this, you have a good chance of holding the brute in your hand for a moment or even getting a picture.

Whether the hook is pulled out, thrown, bent, or just plain broken off so you're left with nothing more than a short piece of leader for your efforts, in the end, the how doesn't really matter. Whether the fish is hard to hook or to land, the difficulty adds to the excitement and the adrenaline rush even if the fish gets away. Frankly, that's what makes the ones you actually get your hands on so special.

The most aggravating way to lose a fish is when you feel the headshake and then the fish immediately runs under your feet. While he zips around in a frenzy within a rod's length of your feet, you frantically thrust your rod straight up into the sky and strip line in a desperate attempt to gather slack. And just as you have it all gathered, the fish darts back into the depths. You feel a slight pull, but the hook is no longer set, and then your line and leader are draped around your shoulders and the hook is set in your hat. If you lose a fish this way, in the presence of a fishing buddy, don't expect sympathy. You'll most likely receive a ridiculing response like, "Stuffed ya, dude!" As Dave Ames so aptly states in his book *A Good Life Wasted,* "Slack is evil!"

I stood head down in awe of the power and speed of the fish that got away. "Nice male," Mark said. "He had to be pushing nine, maybe ten pounds."

No matter how much experience we gain, there will be fish that can make us look like rookies. There was no philosophizing about this loss. The conversation going on in my head was more like George Carlin's seven words you can't say on TV.

After a moment, I looked up at Mark and said with a smile, "I was going to let him go, anyway."

Mark laughed.

I crossed the river, sat down on a rock, and let out a long sigh. I smiled and shook my head when I discovered the bent straight hook. I was simultaneously happy and disgusted. Happy that I had the skills to get a shot at ten-pound steelhead , but disgusted that he kicked my butt.

After a few moments, though, the endorphins were again running rampant, creating that familiar feeling of well-being. *Damn! I love this!* I thought, Win, lose, or draw, the outcome of any single encounter with a fish irrelevant, I loved it all.

Sitting on that rock beside the Cypress River, the thrill of hooking that fish fresh in my mind, I realized just how happy fly-fishing made me. Anxious to relive the feeling, I got out a new hook and began tying it on. That was the milestone marking my addiction. I was hooked!

Chapter 9

The Pursuit of Happiness

Happiness is what life is all about, the pursuit of which, an unalienable right according to our Declaration of Independence. I had effectively journeyed through what Lex described as the three stages of fly-fishing—catching that first fish, then catching many fish, and finally catching big fish—my level of happiness increasing with each stage.

Early in my fly-fishing metamorphosis, I was happy just catching one fish. Landing that first fish on Rock Creek on a sunny summer morning, I was ecstatic. I viewed fly-fishing with wonder and the anticipation of improving my skills.

As my skills improved and my experience increased, catching only one fish no longer resulted in the same level of happiness as that first one. The second stage began, oddly enough, with the rise of a single fish. The time of year and the time of day instantly narrowed the multitude of fly choices to a select few. The fish's rise form looked familiar and further narrowed the possible insects he was rising to take. Even before I saw a bug lifting off the water, I was sure of which fly to select. I can't remember where and when I learned all this. In effect, my knowing which action to take was the result of osmosis, continued exposure to knowledge that I had unconsciously absorbed. My trained mind had mastered the ability to formulate a decision instantly and unconsciously. This process, which Malcolm Gladwell calls "thin slicing," is the theme of his book *Blink: The Power of Thinking without Thinking.*

Gladwell's premise being that with increasing expertise we need less information to formulate a decision and that quick decisions made from limited information are often more accurate than when made with exhaustive of analysis.

Wading into a river and picking up a rock to see what different insects are crawling on it is only one piece of conscious information. Yet from that single piece of information and the collective knowledge gained over the years, the expert fly fisher will chose the correct fly, select the most likely water structure that holds fish and use the best method to deliver the fly to the waiting fish. All of that from looking at the bottom of one rock. That's thin slicing.

Fishing with Pablo on a sunny morning in March in 2004, I stepped into a shallow riffle in the Rush River in Wisconsin, picked up a grapefruit-sized rock and turned it over to examine the underside. Some small nymphs wriggled about, but what got my attention were several one-half inch long, square sided tubes constructed of tiny pieces of woody material. I set the rock down, wadded back to the bank. I handed Pablo a size 16, bright green caddis larva imitation and then I tied one onto my 5X tippet. I put a small split shot weight twelve inches above the fly and set the strike indicator about eight feet above the fly. While Pablo tied on his fly, I walked down to the pool then cast back upstream into the same riffle where I examined the rock and watched as the indicator drifted into the pool. I mended upstream to take the slack out of the line and my indicator stopped in the current. Less than two minutes later, I netted a thirteen-inch brown trout.

I had stepped to the edge of the water, absolutely certain I would hook fish. I can't recall thinking about the most likely location of the trout or how best to reach them. I never once thought consciously about the cast or a mend; I just did it.

Pablo fished the next pool upstream and our catch-and-release melee continued for two hours, and I began to feel guilty over the onslaught. I lost count of the number of trout that I caught and released before finally taking a break to eat my lunch. *So, this is what the second stage of fly-fishing* (catching a lot of fish) *feels like,* I thought. I was very happy.

That day instantly became part of the lens through which I viewed not only past but also present and future experiences. Like any lens, it distorted what I saw. Fly-fishing was never the same for me after that. My expectations had increased dramatically, and I imagined myself reaching that same level of exhilaration each time I entered a new stream or river.

On my first steelhead-fishing trip to Canada in 2007, when I hooked the two fish the first morning and the brute that jerked my rod down the next day, I discovered that my imagination was inadequate to convey the reality. When you catch your first steelhead, you lift your rod and experience a power at the other end of your line like none you've experienced before.

According to Daniel Gilbert, a Harvard psychologist, we can't assign a level of happiness to an experience until we've had that experience nor can we accurately predict how happy a future experience will make us. Looking at a picture of the Grand Canyon is not remotely like standing on the rim gazing at millions of years of erosion. We won't really know what we'll experience or how we'll feel until we get there. The same applies to the thrill of catching and releasing a big steelhead.

Although catching that first fish on a fly rod will always remain a fond memory, it can't match the joy of the first day I chose the right fly and practically unconsciously caught more fish than I could count. And after having my rod tip jerked down into the water by a wild steelhead, hooking a dozen or more ten to twelve-inch trout, although still a hell of a lot of fun, no longer yielded the same level excitement. Those experiences reshaped the lens through which I viewed life.

All those memorable experiences had one thing in common, besides happening while I was fishing. They all happened when another human being was present—not just any human being but one I liked and respected. Although I sometimes enjoy fishing alone, it's the exception, not the rule. Who I fish with is as important as where I fish and what I fish for. Life is too short to fish with pessimistic whiners or hyper-egoed assholes.

As I advanced through the three levels, I discovered that relationships had become an important part of my experiences, more important than I remember them being before fly-fishing.

Fishing is a social activity and has been for thousands of years. According to Wikipedia, tools used for catching fish date to the Neolithic Period, the same period in which agrarian societies began forming and the domestication of cereal crops and animals, including cattle. Apparently, fishing and ranching evolved simultaneously. The Egyptians even chronicled their organized fishing efforts on the walls of tombs and documents.

Sure, I'll go fishing alone if I can't find anyone to go with me, but I'd just as soon fish with others. The need for companionship and cooperation, still essential to human survival, has evolved into a psychological need as well. I contend that a fly fisher's progress—catching a fish, catching a lot of fish, and then catching big fish—are incomplete. I propose a fourth stage: sharing the experience.

This concept of a fourth stage first occurred to me in October 2007 while I was fishing on the Bois Brule River in northern Wisconsin. I was camping alone in the Copper Range Campground on the Brule River, chasing steelhead.

Early fall is spectacular on the Brule. I stepped out from my tent into a landscape painting, trees glowing in their fall colors. Frost covered the ground like pallid chiffon. A chill, from the temperature or the scenery, I'm not sure which, made the hair on the back of my neck stand up. Instinctively, I zipped up the collar on my polar fleece jacket. It didn't help.

I lit a fire, which snapped and popped as it danced from the crumpled newspaper to the dry kindling. The smoke stung my right eye. I reeled back and rubbed it. Damn smoke, I thought.

Soon, the fire crackled into life, throwing flames three feet into the air. I hung the coffee pot on the hook that dangled from a cross bar over the fire. The pot swung as the flames danced around it.

Soon the aroma of camp coffee filled the air and melded with the smoke from the campfire. I attached a new leader to my fly line with the traditional nail knot and then ate a bowl of cereal. As the coffee began to boil, I removed the pot from the hook and placed it on the corner of the picnic table near where I was working. Then, after settling the grounds by pouring a cup of cold water into the coffee pot, I poured myself a cup. I took a sip as I was sitting down to tie on two different-colored stonefly imitations. The rich, nutty flavor of camp coffee tasted better than any coffee brewed at home, or anywhere else for that matter.

The moisture in the air made the beams of sunlight visible as the sun angled through the trees. The cracking sounds of splitting kindling echoed through the campground. Smoke began rising from two other camps. It was time to seek some solitude on the river. I slung my fishing vest over my jacket and attached my net to the ring on the back below the neckline. Rod in hand, I headed to the river.

I had fished for about three hours and had hooked and landed two steelhead earlier. I had time before lunch to work my way down to the nice, big bending run below the bridge near the campground. It was a great hole and I could usually hook at least one steelhead in it. When I got to the hole, a young man in his mid-twenties was fishing in the head.

"Mind if I fish the tail out?" I asked him.

"Not at all," he replied enthusiastically.

"I'm Bryan."

"Steve," he said.

"How long you been here?"

"About an hour," he replied.

He was fishing with floating line and an indicator like me, so I asked, "What've you got tied on?"

"A dark-colored stonefly pattern and a big Prince Nymph," he said. "Is that a good combination?"

"It should work as well as anything," I said. "You might swap the Prince for and egg pattern after awhile."

He nodded but didn't say anything.

"You got any egg patterns?" I asked.

"No," he replied. "Do those work pretty well?"

"They can," I said.

I was still fishing the same stonefly patterns that I'd tied on at the campground. I cast to the middle of the pool and began drifting the tail out. We struck up a conversation as we cast and drifted the hole. He told me that he had gotten married the week before and they had just gotten back from their honeymoon. After the stresses of the wedding, he needed some relief, so he'd decided to drive up from Duluth and spend the day on the river. His wife had agreed that it would be good for him to go.

"She sounds like a keeper to me," I told him.

"She's great!"

I could tell from his casting that he hadn't been fly-fishing long. The rod had not become part of him yet. His mending was slow and deliberate, as if he was still thinking about it.

"How long you been fly-fishing?" I asked.

"Just a couple of years," he said. "I don't normally fly-fish except in Montana."

"You don't fish the Brule much?" I inquired.

"No, I've fished the Brule, just not with a fly rod," he explained. "In fact, I've only caught one steelhead in my life. He was just a small one."

We had fished for about twenty minutes when I thought, *Maybe I'll switch to an egg pattern.* Sometimes, showing the fish something different after you've drifted a hole for a while will trigger a strike, and I knew from experience that the Brule steelhead like egg patterns. I reeled up and was about to grab the fly box containing the egg patterns when I had another thought.

"You want to fish the tail out?" I asked.

"Sure."

When he got down to me, I leaned my rod against some brush and asked if I could look at his bugs. I got out my fly box and handed him a couple of Otter's Soft Eggs that I had tied on #10 egg hooks. "Put those in your box," I said.

"Thanks."

I clipped off his bottom fly and tied on another egg pattern. "I haven't drifted an egg through the tail out yet, so let's see how this one works," I said.

I moved up to the head of the run and began casting up into the choppy, shallow water of the riffle above it. *There's got to be some fish in here,* I thought. I was surprised that he hadn't already hooked one.

"There's one!" Steve shouted.

I snapped my head around; sure enough, he had hooked up. The fish made a couple of nice jumps, slapping water as he came down.

"Nice male," I said.

The fish looked about twenty-five-inches long, a four or five pounder, I guessed. He went to the bottom and stayed there as if he were angry and sulking.

"Get him on the reel and don't let him rest," I advised Steve as I walked past him to position myself downstream with the net. "Lay your rod parallel to the water pointing downstream and turn him perpendicular to the current. Now, he's not going to like that much, so he'll move. If he heads downstream, follow him, but don't walk the dog; take up line as you follow."

The fish made several runs into the deep part of the tail out before he tired sufficiently. Steve led the fish to the spot where I was waiting with the net. I netted the fish, removed the egg pattern from his lower jaw, and then handed the net to Steve. After he handed me his digital camera, I took several pictures, and then he released the fish. He handed me the net while I handed him the camera, then shook my hand.

"Thanks a lot!" he exclaimed.

"I'm tickled to see somebody catch one," I replied. "You did a nice job playing him."

I picked up my rod and walked up to the head of the run. Even though I hadn't caught the fish, I felt the same sense of achievement as if I had. Maybe helping others learn and experience fly-fishing is the fourth stage, the holy grail of fly-fishing. In helping Steve, I had felt the joy that guides and teachers regularly experience on a personal level and fly-fishing writers experience through the occasional chance encounter with a reader who has benefitted from their advice. This gratification is probably one of the reasons they became guides, teachers, and writers in the first place. It sure as hell wasn't for the money.

At this point, fly-fishing gains a purpose, just as the act of fishing and teaching children to fish once served a purpose for Native American tribes in much of North America. The same thing was true for our ancestors in all parts of the world. Fishing was a means of survival for the tribe, for the society.

The experienced fly fisher's contribution to society is to teach less experienced people to fish just as his ancestors did. He's not so much feeding the body as feeding the soul by helping others. Regardless, knowing that they're serving a noble purpose may be why fly-fishing guides are generally a happy lot.

Some of them have quit otherwise satisfactory careers to become fly-fishing guides. Are they trying to fill a hole of some kind? Maybe. Are they seeking to balance the yin and yang of their existence? Could be. Or maybe they're just trying to find a purpose.

I fished with Steve until about lunchtime and then bade him farewell. As I waded across the shallow riffle above the hole, I couldn't get the image of his face, beaming with pride as I viewed it through the camera's viewfinder, out of my mind. The photo represented a milestone in that young man's fly-fishing journey.

Like life, fly-fishing is not about the destination but about hope, anticipation and the experiences along the way. If it were about the fish alone, the stories would always be the same: short, boring, and mostly bullshit. If we allow our lives to become self-centered and materialistic then we can add shallow to the list. The manner in which you travel makes the journey of your life what it is. As the Japanese saying goes, "It is better to travel hopefully than to arrive."

Still somewhat preoccupied with my musings, I passed the deep hole at the bridge, walked up the embankment to the middle of the bridge, and stood staring down at the hole. The recent rains had made the water just turbid enough that I couldn't see the bottom.

A steelhead, probably chasing an emerging insect or a minnow, splashed loudly on the surface of the big hole below the bridge. The water swirled, and I caught a fleeting glimpse of his tail. On most days, I would have stealthily positioned myself to cast to the unwary fish. *He'll be there after lunch,* I thought.

The bright yellow leaves that remained on the maple trees around the hole shone in the midday sun. Tawnier leaves drifted in the light breeze, many falling on the water, floating like tiny boats. The deep crimson leaves of the silver maple held fast to the gently swaying branches. The colors seemed brighter than I remembered.

The hush of rustling leaves caught my attention. Across the pool on the far bank, a tree squirrel carrying a small pinecone bounced through the russet-colored leaves, his bushy gray tail waving like a flag. He stopped two feet from the silver trunk of a sugar maple. Nervously flicking his tail, he looked around with snappy turns of his head. Then he crouched and, with a quick leap, bounced onto the tree trunk, his tiny claws clutching it about three feet from the ground. He paused for a split second and flicked his tail again. In the blink of an eye, he was gone.

I was content just to watch, enjoying some of the infinite pleasures that Nature provides. Suddenly, I was struck by an epiphany: *Fly-fishing is not about the fish.*

Epilogue

What right did I have to cast to a magnificent fish like that hen? True, I was a good student of the game and had worked hard at perfecting my skills. I had embraced the reality that fly-fishing, like life, is about truth and doing the right thing regardless of the consequences. I appreciated its spontaneity and the process of solving the problem of how to catch fish on a fly rod in almost any environment and under a variety of conditions. More important, I respected the sport and the people who played it. And most important, I truly loved it. Casting to that beautiful fish was not a right but rather a privilege that I had earned. I was standing squarely at the crossroads of opportunity and preparedness—success, as I defined it—regardless of the outcome.

I took a long, hard look, concentrating briefly on the hen before moving my concentration upstream where I wanted the cast to land. I raised the rod. Again, my arm tensed—the decisive moment! The hen moved forward about a foot and then dropped back to her original position. *Wait!* I thought. *Something's not right here!*

When the hen moved forward, it looked like she'd grown a foot longer. *Maybe it was just a shadow,* I thought. I raised the rod again. *That didn't look like a shadow.* I lowered the rod, took a step, and leaned forward. My brow furrowed deeply as I strained to extract every detail from the picture. I waited. Then she moved forward again, and I saw it! A second caudal (tail) fin suddenly appeared. It was the male; he had been there the entire time.

My shoulders slumped. The air drained out of me. I was both surprised and sad, disappointed that my efforts couldn't be rewarded.

Ethics are easily compromised in these situations. Spawning fish are very vulnerable and there is no sport in casting to them. Some anglers might consider casting anyway. Even though I was nearly as excited as they were, I would never consider casting to a spawning pair. Doing the right thing regardless of the consequences means not casting, passing on what could be the fish of a lifetime. Accomplishment without integrity—integrity as determined by the actions that we take when no one else is watching—denigrate the value of that accomplishment. Only a sorry bastard would knowingly cast to spawning fish on a redd.

How would I have felt if I hadn't seen the male and had made the cast, jerking that hen off the redd? Sick! The thought made me thankful that I'd seen the male, and disappointment turned to relief. I relaxed, stood straight, and arched my back to relieve the tightness that had accumulated as I watched her.

I moved upstream a little further to see better, then stood there, mesmerized. Although the buck was a nice steelhead by anyone's standards—close to thirty inches—he was considerably smaller than the hen. She dwarfed him, and he had literally remained in her shadow.

Locked in the piscatorial honeymoon ritual, the two fish swayed side by side, simultaneously depositing eggs and milt. Released from my excitement-induced myopia, I could see the dense, creamy white milt sinking onto the eggs as the hen deposited them in the freshly furrowed gravel. Some of the milt and occasionally an egg drifted out of the redd and downstream. Then it hit me like a brick to the head. *The Klamath River!* Thoughts of my original home water came flooding back. Tiny roots reconnected and I remembered what I had learned as a boy in Northern California: If you find a spawning pair of salmon, you'll find trout behind them eating the eggs that drift from the redd.

Snapping my head around, I shot a look into the channel below the mating pair. I stared intently, examining every shadow for the straight silhouettes, parallel to the flow, that expose the fish among the curved outline of the rocks. It took a moment for my eyes to adjust to the dark trough water.

Slowly, the bottom of the trough materialized. *Was that a shadow?* I thought. Just a glimpse at first, but then, about fifteen to twenty feet downstream from the spawning pair, long shadows began appearing. *Shit!* I thought. *They're right there!* Again, my gut tightened. In my previous state, focusing too narrowly on the hen, I had missed these fish completely.

At first, I thought it might be another spawning pair, but the rocks in the bottom were too large for spawning. I took several steps downstream to get the light right, and leaned toward the trough. One by one, like forked flags waving in the current, the moving tails of a close-knit pod of eight steelhead appeared before me. *Unbelievable!*

These fish were smaller than the mating pair, but plenty big enough. Occasionally, one of the fish would dart forward or to the side and then rejoin the group. *That's not spawning behavior,* I thought.

Occam's razor states that the explanation of any observation should contain no more conjecture than is required to explain that observation. More plainly stated, don't get all tied up in your underwear trying to figure things out; stick with the fundamentals. These weren't spawning fish. These were feeding fish.

I reminded myself that steelhead are trout—okay, trout on steroids—and they behave the same way as resident trout do when other salmonids are spawning. Non-spawning fish often congregate just downstream from a spawning pair, waiting to eat eggs that wash out of the redd.

I first witnessed this behavior at twelve years old on the Klamath River in Northern California when the steelhead followed the salmon up from the coast. Both steelhead and resident trout would position themselves downstream from spawning salmon and gorge themselves on the eggs. Spawning fish are off limits—but feeding fish are fair game!

Both hands were now shaking with excitement. With all the pheromones in the water, the fish downstream from the mating pair seemed excited, too, but not especially spooky. One would dart out, grab an egg, and then slip back or turn and rejoin the group. I reminisced about "Rifle Shots at Tortugas," John Randolph's description of George Anderson picking off a line of brown trout feeding along a weed bed in *Becoming a Fly Fisher.* Under these circumstances, how could I possibly miss?

Drifting egg patterns among a pod of trout feeding on newly laid eggs is akin to playing horseshoes; you get points for being close. Their excited state and competition with each other was driving them to move several feet to intercept the eggs washing out of the redd. Exploiting gluttony is easy, regardless of species. The principle of Occam's razor was alive and well; my underwear wasn't the least bit bunched.

I stripped the line in and lengthened the leader under my indicator to about six feet. My anticipation was soaring as I let the current pull the line through the rod guides until it floated straight below me and lifted my rod tip. The tension from the water on the line loaded the rod. I took a deep breath and then snapped the rod forward.

My cast landed ten feet downstream from the mating pair; just as I hoped, they ignored it. A quick upstream mend and the drift headed, drag free, right down the middle of the channel. As my indicator approached the pod, the lead fish shot forward. When he turned back, I ripped the rod downstream. The fish shot straight away toward the alders and then turned downstream, jumping out of the water several times. The spray from the leaping fish glistened in the morning light like a handful of diamonds thrown into the air.

I quickly slapped the edge of the reel spool. What little slack line remained hanging from the reel was gone. It appeared that the fish would keep the fight subsurface, so I began walking downstream while I reeled in line. My biggest concern wasn't landing the fish so much as keeping him from swimming back with the others and scattering them like a handful of copper BBs dropped on a concrete floor. I took him down to the spot where I'd waded up onto the shelf. Now in a little deeper water, the fish made a reel-screaming run out into the main body of the river. I pointed my rod toward the fish at about a forty-five-degree angle to the water's surface and let the stiffer butt section work on him. He settled on the bottom.

The fish lay on the bottom in the faster current, a steady pull on the rod. I took a few steps downstream, laid my rod downstream parallel to the water, and applied enough pressure to turn the fish in the current. He turned and made a run toward me. My gut tightened. I stuck the rod tip in the water, so the line would drag in the water and not go slack, keeping at least some pressure on the hook. I reeled in line as fast as possible as the fish sped back toward me, trying to avoid being "stuffed." He darted past me toward the alders along the shore. The shallower water didn't seem to suit him, so he headed downstream, again taking line from my reel.

The drag on the reel was beginning to exact its toll. As he moved left and then right several times directly below me and then rolled onto the surface of the water, I could tell that he was finally tiring. I held his head up as I walked down to him then slid my net under him.

The gold hook of the Otter's egg pattern had lodged in the roof of his mouth. I quickly extracted it with my forceps. The brightly colored male was in full spawning regalia, his crimson gill plates pulsating as he lay in the net. A wide band of red extended along his twenty-four-inch length. Lowering the net into the water, I reached down, placed my hand under his belly, and lifted him above the rim of the net. Suddenly he regained his wits. With what looked like the slightest effort, he flicked his tail and splashily vanished into the darkened realm of the middle river.

I waded back up to the trough, half thinking that the pod would be gone. I felt a little better when I saw that the mating pair remained locked in the spasms of passion. My breathing remained shallow with anticipation as I approached my previous position on the shelf.

The pod hadn't moved! In the trough, their tails waving against the current, they acted as if nothing had happened. I took a deep breath and exhaled in relief.

Again, my cast landed between the spawning pair and the pod of seven fish. The mend was a little strong, and my indicator moved to the near side of the trough, but it made little difference. Another fish dashed forward and snatched the egg pattern; points for being close. Fish on!

Over the next hour or so—I had no concept of time—I was in nymphing nirvana. Only when the pod was down to three fish did I make a drift that a fish didn't pick up. I didn't land all of them, but I hooked each one even if only for a moment. After releasing the last fish, I looked up and saw that the two honeymooners, seemingly unaware of what had gone on around them, were still consummating their courtship. And that's exactly how it should be.

No, it's not about the fish, but it wouldn't be the same without them.

www.ingramcontent.com/pod-product-compliance
Lightning Source LLC
Chambersburg PA
CBHW031256090426
42742CB00007B/483